# Portraits *of*
# SELF-ESTEEM

**SIXTEEN PATHS TO COMPETENCY AND SELF-WORTH**

# Portraits *of*
# SELF-ESTEEM

## SIXTEEN PATHS TO COMPETENCY AND SELF-WORTH

BONNIE J. GOLDEN

**CENTER FOR APPLICATIONS OF PSYCHOLOGICAL TYPE**

2815 NW 13th Street, Suite 401 ■ Gainesville, FL 32609

800.777.2278 (toll-free USA) ■ 352.375.0160 ■ www.capt.org

Published by
Center for Applications of Psychological Type, Inc.
2815 NW 13th Street, Suite 401
Gainesville, FL 32609
(352) 375-0160

CAPT, the CAPT logo, and Center for Applications of Psychological Type are trademarks of the Center for Applications of Psychological Type, Inc., Gainesville, FL.

Looking at Type is a trademark of Center for Applications of Psychological Type, Inc., Gainesville, FL.

Myers-Briggs Type Indicator® and MBTI® are registered trademarks of Consulting Psychologists Press, Inc., Palo Alto, CA.

Printed in the United States of America.

ISBN 0-935652-62-0

*For Mom, and in memory of Julian and Dad.*

# CONTENTS

## PREFACE

This booklet has been written to help you understand and appreciate your individual personality preferences and differences and to build self-esteem. Self-esteem is an important part of personal effectiveness. When we learn more about our personality preferences through the Myers-Briggs Type Indicator® (MBTI®), we can better utilize our strengths. Working and relating from our strengths leads to increased feelings of competence and self-worth, the major components of self-esteem.

As you read this booklet, you will learn how people who share the same personality type as you find pathways to increased self-esteem. You will also gain insight into situations that may negatively affect it. You will read a story of a person who has increased his self-esteem through type awareness, and you will also learn some strategies for your personal self-esteem enhancement.

You may have taken the MBTI, a psychological instrument to understand your personality preferences. If you have not, or if it has been awhile, a brief review of the preferences is also provided. For a more in-depth overview of Type, refer to *Looking at Type: The Fundamentals* (Martin 1997).

In this book, you will:

- Review the meaning of personality preferences

- Read personal cases as well as testimonials of how type and self-esteem interact

- Learn about the origins of self-esteem

- Examine each of the sixteen MBTI types and expressions of self-esteem for each

- Be provided strategies and resources for self-esteem improvement.

# PART ONE

# A PRIMER TO TYPE AND SELF-ESTEEM

## YOUR PERSONALITY PREFERENCES

It is said that no two people share the same fingerprints. Medical, law enforcement, and detective workers depend on this fact in order to identify each human being uniquely and unequivocally. Yet, there are patterns within groups of people, even though we know each person's print is distinctive. Those patterns include different kinds of loops, whorls, and arches.

Likewise, each individual's personality is unique and special. Still, patterns exist and can be recognized as personality styles and traits. For many thousands of years, philosophers and psychologists have described these patterns and differences. In the early 1920s, the Swiss psychologist and psychiatrist Carl Jung published *Psychological Types* in which he developed his typology of human personality. Later, Katherine Briggs and Isabel Briggs Myers elaborated on Jung's theories, and subsequently Myers developed a practical psychological test to identify personality preferences. Now used around the world, it is called the Myers-Briggs Type Indicator (MBTI).

The MBTI provides a four-part framework for understanding our personality preferences. This framework is an extremely useful tool for us to reach a commonality of understanding about any individual's personality style, while still fully realizing that they will express themselves uniquely.

## THE MBTI® PERSONALITY PREFERENCE SCALES

Extraversion or Introversion, Describing Flow of Energy:

Extraversion (E)

> Your natural energies, perceptions and/or decisions flow outward, toward the world of people and things. You are stimulated by your surroundings.

Introversion (I)

> Your natural energies, perceptions and decisions flow inward, toward the world of thoughts and ideas. Internal processes stimulate you.

**Sensing or Intuition, Describing Information Intake:**

Sensing (S)

> You rely primarily on the five senses to observe the world and gather data. You focus on the present moment and immediate experience.

Intuitive (N)

> You primarily utilize a sixth sense (hunches, connections) to see possibilities that cannot be readily perceived with the five senses. Your perception is beyond the present and includes future events and possibilities.

**Thinking or Feeling, Describing Decision Making Basis:**

Thinking (T)

> Your process of decision-making is based on objective logic and external, observable facts.

Feeling (F)

> Your process of decision making is primarily based on internal values, yours and others,

**Judging or Perceiving, Describing Day-to-Day Style of Life:**

Judging (J)

> You live a planful, schedule-based lifestyle, seeking closure for most tasks and decisions.

Perceiving (P)

> You follow a flexible, spontaneous style of living, without pushing for closure in decisions, tasks, and activities.

The four MBTI scales we have just described are bipolar, and when you receive the results of your instrument, the theory of the test assumes that although we have the eight preferences available within us, one preference of the four pairs is stronger, better developed, and automatically utilized by each person.

Type can be compared to handedness. Although we use both hands to complete tasks, we access our preferred hand (right or left) for tasks that require strength or detail. Access to the preferred is also true for our personality; our preference is more comfortable and automatically takes over.

Furthermore, your four preferences interact in a dynamic way with your information processing (Sensing or Intuition) or your decision making (Thinking or Feeling) function dominating. For in-depth explanations of your preferences, please refer to *Looking at Type: The Fundamentals*, by Charles Martin, or many of the other resources listed at the back of this publication.

## THE COMPONENTS OF SELF-ESTEEM

Self-esteem is your self evaluation, a personal rating. It is essentially a self-acceptance vote.

We base self-esteem on two components: our demonstrated *competence,* which is mostly (although we will see, not entirely) evident in the external world, and *self-worth/self-love,* an internal feeling of acceptance. These two components have separate characteristics; however, self-esteem cannot be sustained by one component alone. Like heredity and environment, both have individual definitions and characteristics, yet they interact with and affect each other.

### COMPETENCE

Competence is the part of the self-esteem equation tied to real-world accomplishments. These are successes that have meaning for the individual as well as to the people in their immediate social circle and to the other subcultures or groups to which the individual belongs.

For Patricia (ESTJ), a 39-year-old computer programmer, her social circles include her husband, her parents and sisters, her co-workers, her

Mexican-American culture, the North American culture, and her professional association. Her career success has provided Patricia with genuine feelings of competence because she does value her work-related accomplishments, and so do the individuals in the social arenas to which she belongs. Patricia can honestly say:

"These are my accomplishments."

"This is what I am capable of."

"This is the challenge I have met."

"Look what I am good at."

Patricia feels and knows that she has indeed demonstrated competence at something meaningful (in this example, career achievement). For Patricia, the work competence side of the self-esteem equation has been achieved.

Fortunately, family, relationships, and culture are positive and healthy for Patricia and her life is in balance. If Patricia's *entire* competence source was work only, she might experience difficulty in retirement or job loss and have a hard time finding other sources of competence and contribution. For example those who heavily focus on relationships may find that their potential self-esteem sources are diminished or ineffective. Tying a sense of competence to only one or two life areas, while neglecting others, leaves self-esteem on tenuous ground. Those types of unbalanced situations are all too familiar to many of us and are more evidence that we should not allow any one area (for example, work, relationships, or athletic ability) to be our single source of self-esteem.

## LIFE AREAS OF COMPETENCE

Patricia was able to experience competence from work and relationships. For adults in the North American culture, the usual life areas in which feelings of competence contribute to building self-esteem are: intelligence, relationships (intimate, family, friends, co-workers) physical self, emotional self, and work.

Throughout our lives, this list will vary. For example, during grade school and high school, athletic ability is an area where competence is important to individuals and their peers, and work would not appear on the list. As adults, unless we are seriously involved in athletics, our performance in that area would not impact our self-esteem as much.

## SELF-WORTH

Self-worth is unconditional positive regard for one's self. This is an internal feeling of value and love, simply because we are human (with all of our assets and failings, our strengths and weaknesses). Our feelings of self-worth are nurtured early in life by our primary caregivers. Acceptance and love from significant others help children feel loved and valued. Children do learn to feel self-respect and self-love if treated with respect and nurtured by love. They are taught from the "all knowing" adults in their lives that they do hold special places in the social system of their families. If they feel valued, they will esteem themselves.

On the other hand, if parents do not acknowledge or accept a child's personality and uniqueness, feelings of unworthiness can occur. Furthermore, continued criticism, constant verbal negativity, and/or physical abuse will create low self-esteem. It is within the first seven years of life that children are most dependent on their primary caregiver's love and approval. Although no one expects parents to be perfect one hundred percent of the time (and parenting mistakes do not automatically equate to children's low self-esteem), damage to children's self-esteem does occur all too frequently if there is on-going emotional or physical neglect, or regular physical, verbal, or emotional abuse.

Therapeutic intervention is required to overcome shaky beginnings. However, precarious self-esteem levels learned from negative childhood programming can be improved. As we will discuss later, this work is a holistic process including examination of internal self-talk, external impact of friends and relationships, and many other factors.

## COMPETENCE AND SELF-WORTH = SELF-ESTEEM

Genuine self-esteem is achieved when we feel competent and successful in the areas of our life that are important to us. Positive achievements, ranging from skilled parenting to successful management of difficult emotions, can elevate our self-worth. Furthermore, if we feel worthy and value ourselves for our unique styles and contributions, we will be attracted to fulfilling or challenging work and healthy relationships. We won't tend to view mistakes and/or failure in those areas as equivalent to global failures as a *human being*.

This relationship between competence and self-worth is often misunderstood. Well-meaning advocates of high self-esteem neglect competence as a critical contributor to our self-esteem. It is not enough for individual self-esteem enhancement to look in the mirror and say, "I love me." We also need to feel we have achieved improvement or success in important life areas for our cultures and ourselves. Again, both competence and that sense of self-worth are essential.

The dynamic of competence and worthiness in action can be observed when successful athletes with few other meaningful interests or relationships are suddenly injured and become depressed; or when the woman who raised children and built a home while her husband was the breadwinner finds herself alone because of divorce or widowhood. She may have no other relationships or areas of competence outside of being a wife or mother.

These sad circumstances are never easy, however those individuals who have core feelings of inherent worthiness can weather the storm of negative changes in their outer lives. Their self-esteem can be restored through gradually achieving competency in new areas. Oftentimes, support groups and counseling are needed to guide their new personal growth process.

## PHILLIP'S STORY

*Nineteen-year-old Phillip (INFJ) was feeling distraught. His girlfriend of two years had abruptly stopped returning calls without explanation. Rather than confront Laura, Phillip simply avoided her around the campus where they both attended college. He knew her schedule; avoidance could be accomplished. But Phillip was deeply hurt because of Laura's rejection. It was stressful not to be able to move freely around campus for fear of seeing his "ex."*

*At work, Phillip had been transferred to a new section of the department store where he had previously performed clerical work in the back office. Now, he was assigned to the customer service area. At that post, he needed to learn numerous forms (to be completed as the customers stood in front of him), operate the cash register, and at the gift counter, wrap a myriad of oddly shaped presents. He immediately felt overwhelmed by the public and fast-paced nature of his new job. Phillip just wasn't catching on to the many details of the forms and procedures he was expected to know. He constantly had to ask other clerks for help, who in turn would become exasperated by Phillip's on-going questions.*

*Finally, by the holiday season, Phillip was so discouraged and negative about his employment situation that he abruptly called in sick one day and never returned. He felt like a failure. Why couldn't he master this job?*

*Phillip continued earning As and Bs in his college classes, but he was depressed. His self esteem, although on shaky ground, was at its lowest point.*

On page 8, you will learn more about Phillip's personality type and how he might evaluate and use his strengths.

## TYPE AND SELF-ESTEEM

Understanding your type is a magnificent tool for self-esteem improvement. Both self-worth and competency can be enhanced once we embrace our strengths and areas of development through type knowledge.

Self-worth is addressed through type when you learn your preferences. The knowledge that all sixteen types have unique and wonderful gifts has been quite an "aha" experience for many of us. As your understanding of type deepens, and as you learn the value and magnificence of your gifts, you will gain a deep appreciation for yourself and all you have to offer to yourself, and to the world.

Furthermore, type insight allows us to clarify and focus on the strengths of our personalities, and apply those strengths in the life areas that are important to us. As successes are achieved through this focus, we shine!

## PHILLIP'S STORY: A TYPE PERSPECTIVE

As an INFJ (dominant introverted intuition) Phillip's job did not tap into his personality strengths from the start. Requiring him to have perfunctory contact with an endless succession of people (many of them in grumpy moods) was extremely taxing for Phillip. His Introversion thrives on one-to-one or small group relationships of depth. The customer service job did not let him exercise his personal strength.

Next, attention to detail and easy grasp of step-by-step procedures are usually strengths of Sensing preferred individuals. Phillip's customer service job was a position that might best utilize the strengths of Sensing types, who more readily focus on the completion of forms, hands-on gift wrapping, and department store policies. As an Intuitive, Phillip was most comfortable in the world of ideas, connections, and big picture processes. Once again, he felt incompetent because he was forced to work with his lesser-preferred, least developed function (Sensing) most of the time.

Lastly, Phillip's Feeling-preferred decision-making style increased his work related stress because he was unable to exercise his personality strength for developing empathic connections with people. Although the clerks in his department were asked to be polite to customers, this job emphasized impersonal, businesslike processes and exchanges of information. At the end of each work shift, Phillip's overall feeling was isolation.

Let's recall Phillip's break-up with his girlfriend Laura. As we will see later, any type can learn assertive behavior. However, some assertive skills may come more naturally to Extraverts than Introverts. Instead of assertively communicating directly with his ex-girlfriend, Phillip kept his feelings inside and avoided confrontation. He also managed to push aside his uncomfortable yet well-justified anger about Laura's behavior toward him.

Even though Phillip's college studies did not suffer during this difficult time, he could not derive much self-esteem from the life arena of education or grades because of his over-emphasis on his relationship with his girlfriend as a self-esteem source.

In summary, Phillip had not learned to appreciate his innate value as a lovable, capable human being, and he allowed the life arena of relationships to be his primary outside source of self-esteem. Furthermore, Phillip did not realize that the customer service job was simply not a match for him. He thought he was incompetent and his lack of success in the life arena of work lowered his self-esteem even further. Insight into type would have helped Phillip see the kinds of work that would use his strengths and therefore be more satisfying for him. Type knowledge might also have led Phillip to seek some assertiveness skills to communicate directly with his girlfriend.

Later, (p. 115) we will see how Phillip finally works through this difficult time in his life.

## THE CIRCLE MODEL

Golden and Lesh (1997) have created a holistic learning model focusing on the complexity of self-esteem sources (see Figure 1). This visual representation, the Circle Model, assists in understanding the larger perspective on contributing factors to our self-esteem. The Circle Model highlights the dynamics of the interactions between an individual's personality and their early upbringing. It also shows the significant contribution of peer groups as well as the overall culture.

The model incorporates psychological type at its core, where inborn personality preferences and other inherited tendencies reside. To learn our natural style at this core through type knowledge gives us information for self-worth and appreciation. Type knowledge also allows us to accept lesser-developed parts of ourselves.

The second circle contains the first social group a child encounters, the family of origin and other caregivers that have an impact in his or her early years. This is the circle closest to the core self, with a major influence on self-esteem development. Our deepest beliefs about our self-worth are formed from relationships with the people in this circle. The second circle can be a source of strength and buffer for the next two circles, or it can be a source of problems. As adults, the second circle contains our current intimate support system including immediate family, partners, and close friends.

The third circle consists of the world immediately outside the home: school, teachers, classmates, and neighbors. These groups have great influence on our self-views, especially starting around age seven. It is then that we begin to compare ourselves to others and rate ourselves accordingly. As adults, this circle can contain work, religious institutions, or other important involvements.

The last circle contains cultural values. The mass media is especially influential in transmitting standards of what is "acceptable" about everything from physical appearance to material possessions.

Studies of adults (Golden 1994, Harter 1989) verify the consistent transmittal of core cultural values for self-esteem in the life areas described previously. Those life area values for self-esteem are delineated on page 12. The information is based on a survey of 300 adults enrolled in community college. Ninety percent of them attended part time and were balancing other life responsibilities such as work and children. The average age of the respondents was 29.8. What specific kinds of experiences and behaviors create feelings of competence and self-esteem in the life areas? On the following page, we see the most commonly occurring responses from this group of adults.

---

**Figure 1**
Model of self-esteem development.

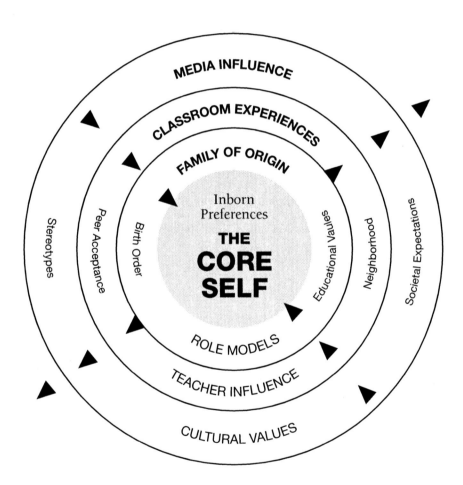

From: *Building Self-Esteem* by Bonnie Golden and Kay Lesh. ©1997. Reprinted by permission of Prentice-Hall, Inc., Upper Saddle River, NJ.

Table 1

# LIFE AREAS: TYPICAL SOURCES OF SELF-ESTEEM

EMOTIONAL SELF

Goals are met ▪ Feelings and ideas are expressed ▪ Positive thinking and self-talk are practiced ▪ Do things for others

PHYSICAL SELF

Feel attractive ▪ Feel attractive for love relationships ▪ Healthy diet ▪ Exercise

WORK

Self-satisfaction, have done one's best ▪ Recognized, praised, appreciated ▪ Helped people and provided good service ▪ Paid well

RELATIONSHIPS (friends, family, intimate, co-workers)

Honesty, Open communication ▪ Feel appreciated and accepted ▪ Feel trusted and respected ▪ Feel true to self and be one's self ▪ Stand firm and speak up ▪ Together, happy, having fun ▪ Pride expressed, accepted, encouraged

EDUCATIONAL PERFORMANCE

Feel "smart" ▪ Grades are good ▪ Praised by teachers ▪ Prepared, study ▪ Participate and contribute

Some common themes are evident in Table 1 regardless of the relationship being examined. For example, *communication* and *respect* are important whether we are discussing, family, friends, lovers, or employers. As we know, respect from significant others in our second circle engenders self-respect. Furthermore, *tangible accomplishments* are also a theme: good grades, a job well done, and a fit body help us to esteem ourselves.

Keep in mind that each of our lists of life arenas may differ. For example, if you are a serious athlete, athletic success might be included as an important life area. Another person's list might include parenting skills. Still another list might include musical performance skills. Many subsets can be generated; however, for most adult individuals in our society this core list will be relevant.

## TYPE PREFERENCES AND SELF-ESTEEM

Do any MBTI preferences have a particular impact on our self-esteem?

Western culture places a high value on Extraverted behaviors: outgoing demeanor and verbal expression, and comfort and ease in interacting with people. Dominant Introverts (like Phillip), who have not developed Extraverted skills, might be seen as shy and too reserved. Additionally, the Introvert's style of processing and pondering before speaking could result in his or her thoughts and feelings being overlooked, suppressed, or ignored because they are not quickly expressed. Of course, it is a challenge to our self-esteem if our thoughts and feelings are not acknowledged.

Furthermore, if we have a "different" style from the dominant operational mode of our families (whether Introverted or Extraverted), and our style is not acknowledged or appreciated, then our self-esteem will be negatively impacted.

Positive feedback might also be lacking for Feeling-preferenced individuals in dominant western culture. Verbal debates and "scientific thinking" are favored values, as well as an emphasis on logic and individual goals. Sensitivity and harmony, the strengths of Feeling types, often are not valued in work and school settings dominated by Thinking values.

It is true that some work environments are attempting to honor and build teamwork and people skills, and we welcome these changes. Additionally, our culture still tends to reward Thinking behaviors in men, and Feeling behaviors in women. Because of these gender differences, individuals whose type preferences are "against the grain" might have a more difficult time finding rewards from the existing social system.

As reported in the CAPT monograph "Self-Esteem and Psychological Type: Definitions, Interactions, and Expressions" (Golden 1994), Extraverts and Thinking types did have higher self-esteem levels than Introverts and Feeling types on the Coopersmith Self-Esteem Inventory. However, once type knowledge is achieved, it provides the opportunity to enhance personal strengths and to learn and address weaknesses in a self-esteem enhancing way. The section "Guidelines for Enhancing Self-Esteem" (p. 111) addresses how we can specifically utilize type as one tool for self-esteem enhancement.

# PART TWO

## THE SIXTEEN TYPES AND SELF-ESTEEM

On the following pages we will examine self-esteem pathways, enhancers, and diminishers for the sixteen MBTI® personalities. Throughout these descriptions are direct typequotes; survey responses* illustrating feelings, thoughts, and events that have contributed to self-esteem enhancement for individuals of the described type. These intermittent quotes are helpful guideposts for how another individual of that type might capitalize on natural skills and areas of competence.

In the section "Talking with . . . ," individual experiences of self- esteem for each type are expressed. The honest sharing of experiences, thoughts, and feelings are candid and insightful and will likely resonate for readers of the same type.

Recall that in the previous section "Typical Sources of Self-Esteem" for life areas, many self-esteem sources are common for all types in our culture. The pages that follow describe the idiosyncratic differences between self-esteem sources for the sixteen types.

*Survey results from more than 300 adult community college students and faculty over a three-year period, mean age: 29.8.

## ISTJ

ISTJs tend to be detailed, fact oriented, and responsible. In their quiet and painstaking way, they can be depended upon. From completing projects (that they feel make sense) to remembering special occasions, once ISTJs believe in people, causes, and things, they can be counted on to persevere in fulfilling their commitments. If ISTJs are willing to reveal their inner thoughts, they can be witty as well as insightful. In new situations they are often reserved and skeptical until the logical value of the situation is proven to them.

### PATHWAYS TO COMPETENCE AND SELF-WORTH

### WORK

ISTJs are often excellent at writing or training others in step-by-step procedures for areas in which they have developed expertise and experience. They have a special ability to break down work systems or methods into their smallest pieces for greater understanding and clarity. Through this detail, others appreciate ISTJs for their competence and knowledge.

For ISTJs, deadlines and projects are to be met and completed. They take their responsibilities very seriously, a practice well appreciated by many supervisors. Because their diligent and steadfast style is often quiet, and could be taken for granted, ISTJs may need to make greater effort to report on their progress and highlight their accomplishments.

> "When my goals are accomplished in a timely manner using confidence, knowledge, and my skills, I feel great."

Once ISTJs become competent in their jobs, they are very stable employees and are secure with their roles in a given organization. However, if changes in an organization begin to occur, especially if those changes do not seem to be based on proven data and facts, ISTJs can lose their equilibrium very quickly and experience distress. Some ISTJs may need to learn to see the big picture and the ebb and flow of change as a constant in itself.

ISTJs choose to reveal little of themselves at work except to a select few whom they trust. Because of the increased emphasis on cross training and teamwork in the workplace, some ISTJs will need to learn to widen their small circles, at least to get projects done or innovations developed.

Some ISTJs might experience difficulty in the theoretical domain. At staff or planning meetings when ideas are expressed and conceptual brainstorming is taking place, ISTJs might feel impatient if the immediate practical application of ideas is not apparent to them.

## RELATIONSHIPS WITH FAMILY, FRIENDS, CO-WORKERS

ISTJs can be counted on to be wonderful commemorators of birthdays, holidays, and anniversaries. Their friends and family are often touched by their great memories of details, such as dates and taste in clothes or books. One ISTJ notes facts about people she cares about and follows up with a loving gesture, such as a gift or hand-made memento. For self-esteem, ISTJs will need to be in relationships in which these actions are appreciated and not taken for granted, or the ISTJ could feel used or even rejected for their efforts.

ISTJs can usually be counted on to be straightforward and succinct about what they think. They will be bluntly honest expressing their opinions to those they trust. Some ISTJs may need to learn to share more intimate *feelings* with those they care about, to further increase the quality of their personal relationships.

ISTJs appreciate and expect consistency and dependability in their relationships, just as they are valued for those qualities by their friends and loved ones. Some ISTJs may need to realize that others' styles of caring may be expressed differently and not as reliably (in their opinion) as their own.

Because ISTJs do not want to initiate change, they may stay in familiar situations or relationships, even if they are unhealthy. More fulfilling and honest interactions with people might pass the ISTJ by because of their reliance on the tried (although not necessarily true). Some ISTJs may benefit from counseling to recognize that they do have other choices in relationships with people.

---

## "I've realized I have three friends who would do anything for me and I for them."

### EDUCATIONAL PERFORMANCE

ISTJs are persevering, steadfast learners. Schoolwork is a domain where ISTJs can excel. Because of their systematic style of processing, ISTJs reliably and thoroughly complete their schoolwork on time or ahead of time.

ISTJ's ease of memory for details and facts serves them well in a wide variety of learning situations. For example, one ISTJ amazes her study partners with her impressive mastery of objective, factual tests requiring memorization. Some ISTJs need to learn to practice finding the theoretical underpinnings and patterns behind the facts that they have mastered. Often, essay tests or theoretical papers require this kind of focus on theory and relationships, and require less focus on facts.

ISTJ frequently look for the immediate application of their learning to concrete experiences in their lives, and as older learners, are often skillful at finding relevance for their educational experiences. Some ISTJs may need to learn to reserve judgment on learning experiences that they don't see as immediately relevant. They might benefit from learning to see the greater value in learning situations that seem questionable to them.

## "I perform all of the requirements for good grades, showing great effort and paying attention."

ISTJs are great at making their own learning schedule and derive feelings of competence from being organized. They often prefer to work this schedule by themselves in order to focus on their plan. However, some ISTJs may need to be encouraged to connect with at least one or two other "study buddies" so they may benefit from other points of view regarding the material they are learning.

### PHYSICAL SELF

Physical fitness is frequently an ISTJ goal to be achieved because fitness makes sense. Scientific data demonstrates for ISTJs the immediate value of physical health. Once ISTJs learn those reasons, they will make a plan to achieve their fitness goals and might reward themselves for doing so!

ISTJs usually prefer individual rather than team sports. They will often keep written records of the details of their physical exercise. Since data keeping comes naturally to ISTJs, they will notice quantifiable results describing their physical improvements. Fitness progress will be a self-esteem source.

ISTJs tend to make positive first impressions because they take great care with the details of their physical appearance. Their socks will match their pants or shirts, their make-up will be fresh and expertly applied; the colors and textures of dress will be a source of pride and acknowledgement from others.

### EMOTIONAL SELF

ISTJs set high standards for themselves. A tendency toward perfectionism can result in severe self-criticism. For self-esteem, ISTJs often need to learn to accept their imperfections since they, too, are fallible human beings.

ISTJs outwardly control their emotions, but inwardly may stew over a fact in a relationship about which they are unhappy. Without talking things through or checking their perceived facts with others they care about, some ISTJs might be blocking true intimacy. Two-way communication can help ISTJs feel some relief from their inward turmoil.

If the outward trappings of happiness (such as position and material acquisitions) exist for ISTJs, they might set aside any emotional unrest or discomfort they may feel. Often, the neglect of their emotional needs can result in physical symptoms or ailments. It is important for some ISTJs to have at least one trustworthy confidant to help ease emotional burdens and provide perspective on a situation.

## TALKING WITH ISTJs

### SELF-ESTEEM ENHANCERS

**When I. . .**

> . . .was hired permanently by the Cable Co. after six weeks of detailed testing to screen people out.

> . . .accomplished what I set out to do. I drove to California with my kids and myself.

> . . .created a procedural manual for my colleagues for a well-received training session.

> . . .learned to read and write in three months to become the smartest child in second grade.

> . . .received a teaching award a couple of years ago. . . it was very important because it acknowledged my work as an adult in my career, not school. I finally made it.

> . . .stand up for myself without losing control emotionally.

## SELF ESTEEM DIMINISHERS

**When I. . .**

. . .don't know what to do or what is expected at work, and then I don't do it right and get reprimanded for it.

. . .let myself down by not doing what I am supposed to do (like homework or studying).

. . .plan for something that does not occur.

. . .am feeling depressed. This depressed feeling of mind often leads to low self-worth.

. . .am not living up to my full potential or at least the full potential for what is expected of adult males.

. . .receive even a hint of displeasure or doubt from a supervisor in how s/he perceives my work performance.

## ISFJ

ISFJs tend to be caring, competent, steadfast individuals. They quietly and diligently proceed to fulfill any obligations they have incurred. ISFJs usually prefer to build close one-to-one relationships with people who have earned their trust. They can be counted on to remember special occasions and are quite kind and sensitive to others' needs.

### PATHWAYS TO COMPETENCE AND SELF-WORTH

### WORK

ISFJs reliably complete tasks assigned to them. They derive satisfaction from getting their work done before or on time. This skill is appreciated and valued in today's work environment.

Step-by-step procedures that require detail and accuracy are areas of strength for ISFJs. They will conscientiously follow whatever is the "correct" way to do things.

---

> ""I always get everything done at work
> that I am supposed to do.""

---

ISFJs enjoy being of service to people. Whether in direct helping relationships or in service to their co-workers, helpfulness is a strong ISFJ value. However, ISFJs sometimes take on more than they should. In their desire to be of service, they may need to clearly communicate their primary responsibilities and learn to decline extra work. For example, one ISFJ supervisor had difficulty delegating even minor tasks to others.

It is important for the health of ISFJs at work to learn to set limits and to assertively communicate them. Self-esteem can suffer for ISFJs if they are feeling unappreciated or at worse used for their extra efforts. Often, physical stress-related symptoms can occur under these circumstances.

Some ISFJs might have difficulty in work situations that require the development of "big picture" concepts such as mission and planning documents. They might need to learn to contribute their unique and realistic ideas, even if they are not seeing immediate, practical purposes for the document or project(s).

## RELATIONSHIPS WITH FAMILY, FRIENDS, CO-WORKERS

Relationships are also opportunities for ISFJs to show their strength of caring for others, through the support and steadfast loyalty and devotion they provide. Self-esteem can occur for ISFJs when they are acknowledged and appreciated for their giving personality style.

ISFJs are cooperative, do not like to rock the boat, and will usually be quite conciliatory if disagreements occur. For self-esteem, it is important for them to surround themselves with people who appreciate them for these characteristics, but who are also willing to support ISFJs for expressing their own needs. They rarely volunteer what they really want.

ISFJs' loyalty and deep caring for people sometimes result in their staying in relationships that are unhealthy for them. For self-esteem they may need a trusted confidant to point out the costs of persisting in one-sided relationships; whether they be at work, with friends, or even family.

---

## "I enjoy helping my friends with their problems."

A skill for self-esteem is assertiveness. ISFJs can learn to honor their thoughts, feelings, and ideas, and to sometimes put themselves first.

## EDUCATIONAL PERFORMANCE

The strong follow-through skills of ISFJs usually make them accomplished students. Academic achievement can become a fine source of self-esteem because of this.

ISFJs enjoy learning from teachers who seem to care about them. Personalized comments or a personal relationship with educators motivate ISFJs to do well. ISFJs usually like to please their teachers. Some ISFJs may need to learn to focus more on the material to be learned than being concerned with the establishment of a teacher/student relationship, especially if it is impractical for one to occur.

Learning goals are important to ISFJs and so is a learning structure. When they know what is expected of them, they will methodically set out to finish their academic responsibilities.

ISFJs are frequently strong at learning facts and details, especially if those facts and details relate to human or helping applications. They may have more trouble with abstract concepts and requirements.

---

"I learn best when things are at a more personal level; and when learning is hands-on."

## PHYSICAL SELF

The best strategy for ISFJs to succeed in physical and mental self-care is to schedule these activities as a task to be done, because ISFJs are usually quite responsible for fulfilling any commitment they make.

However, ISFJs tend to be less committed to their own needs, and so it can sometimes be difficult for them to make time for themselves; they often do not prioritize time for activities that are for their own benefit.

For self-esteem, it is crucial for ISFJs to practice good self-care habits. To this end, they may need to be shown the factual cost of neglecting their own health. They can easily burn out or become ill and be doubly frustrated if they are unable to help others because they haven't first cared for themselves.

## EMOTIONAL SELF

ISFJs are caring people. They demonstrate their caring through action, and are dependable and quite sensitive on the inside.

Because their true feelings or preferences are not readily verbalized, ISFJs tend to worry and stew, instead of expressing or at least checking out some of their fears or conclusions. They can also become overextended, not quite realizing their own limits.

To keep them from becoming overwhelmed, used, or even abused, it is vital for ISFJs to learn assertiveness skills. Setting limits, saying no, verbalizing both positive and negative feelings are skills that can be learned with practice and patience. Assertive behavior for ISFJs does not mean they have to compromise their essential, caring selves.

## TALKING WITH ISFJs

### SELF-ESTEEM ENHANCERS

When I. . .

> . . .do things for others out of the blue when they least expect something.

> . . .am told by a teacher how well I'm doing in her class.

> . . .am told by people that I've helped them (in one form or another).

> . . .feel good about helping others by explaining with patience.

> . . .am enjoying my friends and colleagues at work.

> . . .get my report card—all *As*.

### SELF-ESTEEM DIMINISHERS

When I. . .

> . . .am treated disrespectfully; as if the person thinks I am beneath them.

> . . .get into an argument.

> . . .don't get calls from my friends.

> . . .don't get acknowledgement of personal qualities from people around me.

> . . .get intimidated by someone yelling at me.

> . . .get nagged to do the things I already know need doing.

## INFJ

INFJs tend to be creative and visionary, and enjoy developing distinctive models and solutions for problems and issues that affect the lives of people. They want to make a unique difference in whatever area captures their interest and imagination. INFJs are loyal and caring toward the people they trust, although they may not verbalize their feelings. They strive to make their ideas real, in almost any area.

## PATHWAYS TO COMPETENCE AND SELF-WORTH

### WORK

INFJs are energized by work that allows them to create ideas for solving problems, implement those ideas, and be recognized for their unique contributions. They enjoy pioneering and making their mark in a positive way.

---

> "My self-esteem is high at work when things are going well. The guests are happy, problems solved, and I'm rewarded for good work."

INFJs need time and space to read, think about and/or write out their plans and visions. Too many interruptions or not enough time to introspect will drain the INFJ of energy or effectiveness.

INFJs do want to work collaboratively and non-competitively with others. Because of their deep caring for people, it is best for them to balance people contact with solitary time. For self-esteem and job satisfaction, those conditions are optimal.

If a position has too much structure, procedures, or details, INFJs will begin to feel stifled, and at worst incompetent. Self-esteem can suffer when they are drained by the extra effort they need to exert to master procedures and details.

INFJs want implementation and closure. They will work tirelessly to bring their projects to fruition. However, others may feel shut out by their single-minded pursuits (although this is not the INFJ's intent). Sometimes their visions do not coincide with the bureaucratic or political realities of a work situation. Self-esteem at work can suffer for INFJs if they are unable to integrate those realities into their visions.

## RELATIONSHIPS WITH FAMILY, FRIENDS, CO-WORKERS

INFJs highly value their friends. They have often developed relationships over a long period of time. One INFJ points out that she prefers to focus on the quality of the interaction with her friends and not the quantity of times she sees them or how many friends she has.

In turn, INFJs really want to be understood and appreciated for themselves. Because they focus on big picture questions, they sometimes have difficulty communicating their thoughts to others. However, when they find like-minded souls, they relish the relationship.

---

## "I feel satisfied when I feel like I've made a difference in someone's mood."

INFJs want peaceful conditions at home and at work. They seem to have special antenna for others' moods and feelings. They are also deeply sensitive and can sometimes overreact or over interpret another person's behavior as negative or critical toward them. For self-esteem, INFJs may need to learn objectivity to determine if their interpretations are accurate.

Other types may interpret the INFJ's needs for solitude as aloofness. INFJs could be hurt if their style is misinterpreted in a negative way. Some INFJs may need to make extra efforts to connect and communicate with others in order to maintain their self-esteem support system.

## EDUCATIONAL PERFORMANCE

INFJs enjoy the process of learning for its own sake, and when captured by new subject matter, they will thoroughly explore it. They can quickly develop expertise and perform well on learning tasks.

In school, INFJs enjoy independent learning, reading, and writing. They gravitate to the library or computer, and want a peaceful environment in which to concentrate. Some INFJs may need to connect with others as study buddies or in study groups. They may miss important facts or perspectives if they rely only on their personal understanding of an idea or concept.

The academic setting or workshop can be a "second home" for the INFJ. Learning related to their goals or that is focused on human accomplishments or the betterment of humanity will most capture their interest. They will have a more difficult time with rote subjects that require step-by-step details. If motivated by an instructor or classmate with whom they've connected, these subjects can also be mastered by INFJs for self-esteem enhancement.

---

> "I like receiving approval from teachers and praise from teachers and peers."

INFJs will usually meet deadlines and thoroughly finish every aspect of their assignments. These skills are crucial for academic success, and INFJs can derive a strong sense of self-esteem from their fit with the academic environment.

## PHYSICAL SELF

INFJs can meet their health goals if they make them a priority. If their exercise time is scheduled, they will more likely be committed to carrying out their plans. INFJs often prefer individual activities or those in small groups such as tennis, walking, golf, hiking, or bowling.

Because of their voracious reading habits, INFJs will learn the health benefits of nutrition and exercise. Thus, knowledge of the benefits of healthy habits can be motivating for INFJs.

INFJs can sometimes undereat or overindulge if they neglect "outer world" self-care for too long. Self-esteem and physical health can suffer when this happens.

## EMOTIONAL SELF

INFJs are usually profoundly in touch with their emotional reactions. This fine characteristic and gift creates sensitivity to others as well. For self-esteem, it is important for INFJs to discern which feeling reactions they want to spend time exploring and which ones they may need to logically detach from. This discernment can save them energy from worry and anxiety and help them to let go of issues over which they have little or no control.

Assertive expression of feelings and thoughts will help INFJs in their communications with others. Skills such as giving and receiving feedback and asking for help are important aspects of assertiveness. INFJs sometimes tend toward perfection and thus can be very guarded about sharing their questions, ideas, and visions.

Overload from the outer world can create irritation and sometimes anger for INFJs. For relationships and their own mental health, it is important for INFJs to ensure that they engage in a balance of activities alone and with others. They may need to develop the assertiveness skill of limit-setting.

## TALKING WITH INFJs

### SELF-ESTEEM ENHANCERS

**When I. . .**

> . . .can feel trust and closeness with my boyfriend and we have a good time together.

> . . .am very involved and focused on something new.

> . . .am accepted for what I am. When I am complimented, praised, or receive approval.

. . .can make people laugh. When they find me amusing.

. . .don't compromise myself.

. . .am in control of work, school, and personal responsibilities.

## SELF-ESTEEM DIMINISHERS

**When I. . .**

. . .feel that people don't/can't make the time to be with me.

. . .am yelled at by my manager, and he doesn't realize how much work I really do.

. . .seem to be doing all the favors: driving, cleaning, helping, complimenting.

. . .have to ask a lot of questions and make stupid mistakes.

. . .when I am betrayed by friends I have helped and trusted.

. . .question myself. Don't trust myself.

## INTJ

INTJs are determined, logical, innovators who enjoy creating new under-standings for old situations. They often appear serious and reserved and their internal thinking process may not be obvious to others. INTJs can be vision-ary and very thorough in fleshing out their ideas in order to bring them to fruition in the external world.

### PATHWAYS TO COMPETENCE AND SELF-WORTH

### WORK

Achieving competence is an overriding drive for INTJs. Competence is inherently satisfying. Additionally, appearing competent to others is gratify-ing, so a self-esteem enhancing feedback loop can occur for INTJs when they are performing well.

Sharing their big picture ideas with managers, supervisors, and other co-workers can be an important contribution for INTJs. They are visionary and can excel at long-range goals, perspectives, and plans.

---

### "I feel great when a new idea of mine works and I can watch it be implemented by others' who also like my idea."

Intuitive insights can be creatively rewarding for INTJs. Furthermore, INTJs like to achieve specific goals and feel rewarded when their insights lead to identifiable accomplishments. They are rarely content to simply let their ideas for improving work simmer in their head. They want to create outside action to improve whatever project or situation on which they are focused.

INTJs need to be careful presenting visions and insights. To some, INTJs can appear threatening or difficult to approach because of their firmly held beliefs and opinions.

Satisfying careers are those that allow INTJs to create and implement original ideas and connections, to work with systems, and to work with people who provide respect and who are respected by them. Their strength tends to be logical analysis, although they may have a harder time mastering details.

## RELATIONSHIPS WITH FAMILY, FRIENDS, CO-WORKERS

Participation in engaging discussions about ideas, theories, and connections can make INTJs stimulating company. They can usually be counted on to express a well-thought perception regarding the topic at hand.

INTJs are much more approachable and open on the inside than might appear on the outside. They may need to learn ways to outwardly express that they are available for engaging with others and invite others to connect with them.

---

> "I am quite reserved, yet with people I trust and respect, I am able to open up quite a bit."

INTJs naturally critique and analyze. They might need to consciously focus on the pluses and positives of a person or relationship so others are not discouraged by the INTJs objective style.

Small talk often seems wasteful to INTJs. Some may need to push themselves a bit and be willing to engage in social niceties at work or family events. INTJs need to create smoother relationships with their partners, families, and/or co-workers.

## EDUCATIONAL PERFORMANCE

Because of their drive to learn and get the "big picture," academic learning for INTJs is often pleasurable and something to master.

INTJs are thirsty for knowledge. Reading, problem solving, and researching come naturally; grades and other kinds of results are usually outstanding.

---

### "I feel very gratified when I know I've mastered a subject."

---

INTJs prefer to chart their own learning course, and self-paced learning is a natural talent.

INTJs have a more difficult time with details and numerous facts and need to slow down their devouring of information in order to pay attention to specifics that may be important to others or the task of learning.

## PHYSICAL SELF

INTJs may tend to neglect physical or fitness pursuits because so much of their "action" is in their heads. Often, when they pursue physical activities, they prefer less competitive forms, unless they are competing with their own best self.

To achieve balance, INTJs can read about the scientific benefits of fitness, nutrition, and holistic health, and this evidence will often serve as the initial motivation to commence physically beneficial pursuits.

Once INTJs see concrete evidence of the benefits of physical or outdoor activities, they will honor their physicality and find healthful activities inherently rewarding.

## EMOTIONAL SELF

Since INTJs' dominant force is internal, they often upset themselves when mistakes occur in the external world. For example, one INTJ manager was personally mortified when he lost a purchasing form and questioned his entire competence level until he located it. INTJs can learn to laugh a bit more and also ask for help from others for "hands-on" organizational skills.

INTJs high standards and reliance on competence cause them to be acutely self-critical. INTJs may need to develop the "courage to be imperfect" and accept their fallibility.

Often, INTJs need to learn to share feelings once they establish trusting relationships with people who accept them. Additionally, increased communication can provide reality checks for their sometimes-skewed internal picture of the world. INTJ's distortions may happen if their interpretation of feelings or events have been held inside too long, and not provided a reality check.

## TALKING WITH INTJs

### SELF-ESTEEM ENHANCERS

When I. . .

> . . .received a scholarship to the University.

> . . .received rank promotions in my martial arts class.

> . . .got a job that I felt matched my potential and expertise.

> . . .graduated from high school with high honors.

> . . .had a scientific paper published on lab work I did.

> . . .follow through on goals I set like finishing my work and eating the right foods.

### SELF-ESTEEM DIMINISHERS

When I. . .

> . . .am degraded about my work.

> . . .do something good and nobody notices it.

> . . .am criticized about something I've created.

> . . .share something personal and someone misunderstands or judges me poorly by it.

> . . .think too much about things I would have said or done better.

> . . .am made to feel that my ideas or actions are inferior or wrong.

## ISTP

ISTPs are down-to-earth pragmatists. They enjoy pursuing the hobbies and interests that fulfill their need for excitement, physical challenge, or that capture their attention. They want the time to do so at pace and in a style of their own. ISTPs are cool problem solvers and often find expedient solutions in crisis situations. ISTPs have a fun-loving, teasing aspect to their personality; however, this is only shared with those with whom they trust and are comfortable.

## PATHWAYS TO COMPETENCE AND SELF-WORTH

### WORK

Optimum, esteem-enhancing work situations for ISTPs are those that provide immediate, tangible results, and/or provide them the time and space to solve problems.

Schedules are frequently resisted by ISTPs, since they prefer to work according to their own internal clock with bursts of energy. Since working within organizations often implies scheduling, for maximum competence, ISTPs will need to adjust to organizational demands for scheduling in order to gain work self-esteem.

---

> "I do a good job and know I have, no matter what anyone else thinks."

ISTPs frequently have hands-on or technical interests, from computers to jewelry making. For feelings of competency and job satisfaction, a job needs to express those interests. One ISTP manager who worked in a bureaucracy began watercolor painting and used this hobby as energy replenishing time to provide balance to her bureaucratic work setting.

ISTPs have a knack for organizing details in their heads and are consulted by others in areas where they can show this expertise. They are usually quite open to sharing information if it relates to their niche.

Frequently, ISTPs who are not well matched to their work will have a difficult time dealing with bureaucracy or deadlines. They may give short shrift to projects they just want to get out of the way. For competence to occur, ISTPs need to learn better time management skills and persist until completion.

## RELATIONSHIPS WITH FAMILY, FRIENDS, CO-WORKERS

ISTPs are often quite easy-going and matter-of-fact in their relationships. They enjoy sharing activities and information with other people.

ISTPs can be generous in their concrete actions toward people. They will often give presents and like to indulge the children in their lives.

---

> "I am able to pick my friends up when they're depressed, enjoy humor with them, and give advice."

ISTPs do not tend to verbalize feelings and prefer not to discuss others' feelings either. Others may feel their ISTP friend is unapproachable, and become frustrated since ISTPs often give few nonverbal cues. As ISTPs mature, they can learn to share feelings a bit more for more fulfilling relationships.

Key for ISTPs in relationships with others is to maintain their freedom. They do not want to feel cornered or boxed in.

## EDUCATIONAL PERFORMANCE

Logical, factual, and relevant material will motivate ISTPs in educational or training experiences. They prefer learning that can be immediately applied in an area that has captured their interest.

ISTPs learn best through sensory experiences, whether through physical practice or perhaps using the computer as a learning tool.

Theory that is perceived as irrelevant by ISTPs will cause them to tune out and become intolerant of the class or training session. They may need assistance from a friend or tutor in order to make the connection between theory and application.

In a program of learning/study, ISTPs may need to make the effort to negotiate deadlines and self-paced learning contracts with the instructor. This less structured process can provide the ISTP with a feeling of competence and control to help their self-esteem in the educational setting.

## PHYSICAL SELF

ISTPs usually take pleasure in athletics. They enjoy the physical sensations of being involved in something invigorating that is of interest to them. They might become quite adept at sports for their own satisfaction, although they are rarely competitive.

Unless fitness and nutrition are of interest to the ISTP, they usually pay little attention to structured diet or exercise schedules. They do not want to be nagged or told what to do.

Self-care is a self-esteem issue, and it sometimes takes an authority figure (e.g. physician) or health crises, for the ISTP to take action and make healthy habits a priority.

## EMOTIONAL SELF

Under normal circumstances, ISTPs are fairly unaffected by emotions, anxiety, or fears. They will stay rather cool, even in extreme conditions.

——————————————

## "I don't allow my inner thoughts and feelings to lower my self-esteem."

Under stress, usually when feeling pressured or boxed in, ISTPs might withdraw further into their shells, and even feel sorry for themselves. Others may not know this is happening through verbal cues; however, they may detect a change in the demeanor of the ISTP that borders on petulance.

As with all types, a trusted significant other or counselor can help them logically analyze events. ISTPs may need guidance in seeing nuances and other possibilities in a situation. Some ISTPs might especially need to learn focus on their Feeling function, as their feeling reaction is often pushed aside or ignored. This strategy might bring the ISTP back to equilibrium.

## TALKING WITH ISTPs

### SELF-ESTEEM ENHANCERS

When I. . .

   . . .enrolled in college when I didn't have support from my family.

   . . .do well and get complimented for my hobby-painting.

   . . .see how proud my parents were of me graduating from high school.

   . . .was promoted to manager after working at my job for two years.

   . . .don't have to depend on someone else for total support: example, having a boyfriend or husband to take care of me.

   . . .got the highest grade in my history class.

### SELF-ESTEEM DIMINISHERS

When I...

   . . .do not achieve the goal I was striving for.

   . . .am put down by someone who doesn't understand me.

   . . .don't know anyone and I have to mingle with strangers.

   . . .didn't go out for the football team but wanted to.

   . . .do poorly on essay tests.

   . . .am surrounded by family problems and they expect me to solve them.

## ISFP

ISFPs are often quiet, unassuming, and modest individuals. They hold a deep caring for people and living things. They are extremely sensitive and in touch with the feelings of the people around them. People who get to know ISFPs discover their delightful and surprising sense of humor. ISFPs would rather go-with-the-flow and let life reveal itself, than to plot and plan.

## PATHWAYS TO COMPETENCE AND SELF-WORTH

### WORK

For ISFPs, work needs to be congruent with their deeply held values of helping and respecting others. Whether in a nonprofit organization or a business they feel is worthwhile, ISFPs will feel best if these values are expressed.

ISFPs work well when they know what their specific responsibilities are and what is expected of them. However, within those expectations they prefer to have the latitude to pace themselves in a low-key way. They will get the job done at their own pace and style.

It is important for ISFPs not to feel pressured in their work setting from intense and unremitting deadlines or from strife. Because they tend to internalize anything they perceive as critical of them, they will have a difficult time maintaining self-esteem when there is stress in an organization. Even if it appears that it shouldn't affect them, it does!

---

> "Work is best when I don't make mistakes and when customers don't upset me."

ISFPs enjoy organizing and do well with concrete details. They enjoy providing the classification system for categorizing items such as newspaper clippings, bookkeeping, or file systems. Self-esteem and pride occurs when they see the results of these efforts.

ISFPs are often refreshingly unpolitical. They are not trying to seek promotions, however they do need recognition as well as reward and fairness from their superiors. If that quiet appreciation is not forthcoming, their self-esteem will suffer.

## RELATIONSHIPS WITH FAMILY, FRIENDS, CO-WORKERS

The healthiest relationships for ISFPs are those in which they can express themselves in small groups or on a one-to-one basis. With this opportunity, others deeply appreciate their lovely sensitivity and their surprising senses of humor.

ISFPs often relate well with small children or people less fortunate than them because they are so accepting and understanding. As parents they are not likely to be extremely directive. However, it is crucial for the ISFP's sense of self-esteem that they are not dominated by anyone. They often recoil and retreat if hurt, and this can be deeply damaging to their worth.

Others tend to confide in ISFPs. They are often fine-tuned listeners, sympathetic and nonjudgmental. Through this quiet support, the people they become close to know they can trust them and count on them. Again, it is important for the ISFPs sense of self to have equal time being heard.

ISFPs generally are fun-loving and easy to like. They prefer to remain neutral in conflict and have great anxiety if they sense something didn't go right. For their self-esteem and emotional survival, emotional detachment skills need to be developed by many ISFPs, so they are not consumed by worry.

---

"I like when my family praises me for doing things well and tell me they are proud of me."

## EDUCATION PERFORMANCE

ISFPs often prefer to learn about subjects and participate in classes that are practical and hands-on, either in the service of life (people, children, animals, the environment) or in services that have immediate, practical applications. Abstract theory does not often capture the attention of the ISFP.

Memory for details can be a strength of ISFPs. They will invent unique organizing and classifying systems for their learning material. One ISFP is quite an enjoyable study partner because he likes to invent humorous mnemonics for learning new subject matter.

For optimal learning to take place for ISFPs, the educational environment needs to be accepting and tolerant of their processing style. Impatience and negative criticism will frequently cause the ISFP to shut down from anxiety, and they could become very negative toward themselves and the educational experience.

Real life examples and situations to which the ISFP can relate will give life to learning. Additionally, visual and audio materials as well as hands-on lessons are critical.

## PHYSICAL SELF

For fitness goals, ISFPs usually prefer activities they can do alone or with one or two other people. ISFPs are frequently involved in walking, gardening, or golf, for example. It is uncommon for an ISFP to take part in anything competitive, however they often like to observe sports.

Internal equilibrium is crucial for ISFPs' self-care. If they are in a hurt state, they may neglect their own physical or nutritional needs. It is important for them to have connections with caring family or friends who will help them stay on track, healthwise.

ISFPs prefer to be spontaneous, so any commitment to a fitness and health regime will often take extra effort for them. Again, an encouraging friend to gently help them adhere to their plans is important because the ISFP will often put their own needs last.

## EMOTIONAL SELF

ISFPs' gift of sensitivity is a double-edged sword. ISFPs' sensitivity to others' feelings also makes them susceptible to internal scrutiny that easily turns into self-criticism. In many ways, they personify the phrase "own worst critic." For self-esteem, ISFPs especially need to learn to monitor their negative and irrational self-talk. Some ISFPs might need counseling to assist them in developing Thinking based analysis and objectivity.

---

## "I'm a good person and know I am. It's nice when people tell that."

Taking a few more risks, especially by sharing their thoughts and feelings and by engaging in activities in the outer world, can build self-esteem for ISFPs. A trusted friend or counselor could point out that risking means mistakes are made and that mistakes are OK.

The skill of assertiveness is extremely important for ISFPs. Their sweet-naturedness lends itself to easy domination by others. Learning to set limits and boundaries is key to protecting the selfhood of the ISFP.

## TALKING WITH ISFPs

### SELF-ESTEEM ENHANCERS

When I. . .

> . . .ceased friendships with people who were disrespectful toward me.

> . . .lost weight and felt like I was doing something with my life.

> . . .gave birth to my children.

> . . .got my GED.

> . . .complete my assignments at work and am positively acknowledged for them.

> . . .encouraged my mom to attend college.

## SELF-ESTEEM DIMINISHERS

**When I. . .**

. . .have a fight with someone I know.

. . .get embarrassed in front of a big group of people.

. . .have to speak in front of class.

. . .am ignored by my kids.

. . .feel I don't know how to do something.

. . .stay at home and don't get dressed up nicely. Just kind of lounge around.

## INFP

Deeply held, people-driven values motivate INFPs. They have varied interests and enjoy creating and exploring the connections and nuances around those interests. INFPs are loyal and supportive friends and have an enjoyable sense of humor that they share with those they trust. INFPs desire to contribute to people and the world and seek unique ways to change theirs and others' lives for the better.

## PATHWAYS TO COMPETENCE AND SELF-WORTH

### WORK

INFPs tend to seek career paths in which they can impact human development through a variety of means. Self-esteem occurs when INFPs can contribute through writing, encouraging others through teaching or counseling, or generally through being quiet catalysts for human development.

INFPs often prefer to pursue work in solitude or with one or two others that have earned their trust. Some INFPs serve as volunteers or on boards in which they can contribute to causes for which they feel passionate. INFPs not involved in these ways can seek self-esteem competence by doing so.

---

## "It is crucial for me to get in touch with myself and work for my goals, not someone else's goals."

Because INFPs usually are reserved within a work environment, individuals who are domineering or vocal might overlook their contributions. However, INFPs do appreciate recognition from those they respect, and for this to occur, they may need to learn some skills in drawing attention to their accomplishments.

Typical bureaucratic organizations with impersonal chains of command will alienate most INFPs. Because INFPs tend to be more spontaneous and creative, they could experience such organizations as stifling and demoralizing. INFPs may find it difficult to conform to too much structure. For self-esteem, some INFPs may need to find either individuals within a workplace who value their style, other settings to contribute their uniqueness, or look for ways to change careers.

INFPs focus on many interests and internal visions. Their action takes place internally with their own timelines. This can be an issue for others who misunderstand the INFP style. In order to further projects with co-workers, some INFPs may need to show details and concrete results in order to be valued and appreciated, or their unique vision can be overlooked.

## RELATIONSHIPS WITH FAMILY, FRIENDS, CO-WORKERS

INFPs are loyal, warm, and dependable friends. They are steadfast in their valuing of others whom they trust, and those whom have earned this trust can count on a fulfilling and giving relationship.

Often, others at work or in socially oriented situations see INFPs as reserved, shy, or even cool. Their deep internal process and sensitivity is not easily revealed, and their personal style can be negatively misinterpreted. Although their natural preference is for deep and longer lasting relationships, some INFPs might need to make a special effort to touch base with others on a more casual basis.

INFPs typically derive joy from the natural wonder and nonjudgmental style of young children. They are wonderful nurturers of their own or others' children. For example, when one INFP gave a baby gift to her close friend, she made sure to give a small gift to the six-year-old brother, knowing he might feel overlooked.

INFPs usually enjoy entertaining people whom they care about and will often bake or cook and create an ambience for their loved ones to feel special. This knack for helping others feel special is a rare skill for which INFPs can feel proud. They may overlook this quality in themselves because it is so natural to them.

## EDUCATIONAL PERFORMANCE

INFPs are attracted to concepts and theories and like to make connections to their own values and life experience when studying. They often excel in writing papers. Some INFPs may need to work harder at noticing or memorizing details, as well as logically analyzing and dissecting their learning material.

Some INFPs, because they are very value driven and concerned with relevance to people and their values, may become impatient with work or schooling that requires studying impersonal, factual material. For self-esteem, INFPs need to reward themselves for getting through these kinds of learning experiences.

INFPs can be motivated by personal relationships with their teachers. Although they often do not share in class, INFPs might seek personal connection to their teacher through office meetings and conversations. Although the material may not motivate the INFP, the teacher/student relationship can encourage their success.

---

> "It's important to me to receive top grades from work well done and to get praise and compliments from the teacher."

INFPs will delve deeply into subjects that interest them and are energized by the process of learning. Because many learning situations necessitate concrete products with deadlines, some INFPs may need to adapt by creating an "imperfect" product (by their own standards), to meet educational requirements.

## PHYSICAL SELF

Since caring and connections with people inspire INFPs, some will more consistently pursue fitness goals if they can walk with a partner and talk. They will often be as committed to not letting down their workout partner as to their own fitness! One INFP hired a personal trainer at a health club. In this way, she not only became fit and lost weight, but she did so through a one-to-one relationship.

INFPs often enjoy caring for animals and become physically active when playing with their animals or taking them for walks.

Physical or sports oriented pursuits are more likely for INFPs if they are in a small group or one-to-one activity (such as tennis or golf). Most INFPs dislike competition and would rather take part in solitary or cooperative physical endeavors.

## EMOTIONAL SELF

The saying "still waters run deep" is especially true for INFPs, who feel and intuit their own and others' needs quite easily. INFPs tend to take this sensitivity for granted. Recognizing it as a gift can boost self-esteem.

INFPs are pleasant company and enjoy their friends and family immensely. Because INFPs often do not like to "rock the boat," they will avoid conflict or sometimes avoid expressing their opinions. Stifling their feelings and opinions can lead to lowered self-worth for INFPs because their needs become overlooked. The skill of assertive communication is important for INFPs' emotional health and self-esteem.

Communication in general for some INFPs is a stumbling block. Their sensitivity is a strength, yet often times they will negatively interpret people's motives or behaviors and can take others by surprise if they have been angered by a previous occurrence. For self-esteem, increased communication will lead to more intimate and healthy interactions.

---

"I'm at my best when I accept myself, all my great points and my not-so-great points."

## TALKING WITH INFPs

### SELF-ESTEEM ENHANCERS

**When I. . .**

. . .know my family loves me and cares about my achievements.

. . .am encouraged by my boss, parents, or teachers.

. . .do a good deed.

. . .made the decision to be more assertive/less passive in certain specific situations in my life and held to my decision.

. . .help friends.

### SELF-ESTEEM DIMINISHERS

**When I. . .**

. . .am questioned or challenged by people who don't seem to take me seriously as an individual/adult.

. . .have my trust betrayed.

. . .am embarrassed for whatever reason in front of others.

. . .am ignored.

. . .talked down to by someone.

. . .don't get approval from my parents.

# INTP

INTPs are probing and logical analyzers. They most ingeniously apply this style of analysis to small and large problems. Through their in-depth scrutiny they often provide insights to a situation that almost no one else might see. INTPs appear fairly reserved unless they are discussing a topic for which they feel excited. They are most interested in ideas, yet less in the implementation of those ideas in the outer world.

## PATHWAYS TO COMPETENCE AND SELF-WORTH

### WORK

INTPs can shine at work when they are able to create or solve problems independently. They do not have the need to control a project, but they are best when they are working with others whom they respect intellectually, no matter what their position in the organization's hierarchy.

INTPs are energized by their internal mental discoveries. On projects that they are interested in, they will learn everything they can. Oftentimes they might reorganize their learning into a new model that is logical and often quite brilliant. For competency, INTPs need the time and space for this research-oriented mental process to occur. One INTP, when frustrated with his particular work situation remarked, "Don't they understand that we need to be paid to think?"

Process, not product, is the orientation of INTPs. However, many work sites require "product," and some INTPs may need to learn skills in implementing their ideas.

Because of their terrific ability to distill and summarize problems and issues, often INTPs are consulted and respected by co-workers for their insights.

# "My co-workers respected me and my work so much that I was elected union president."

INTPs need freedom in their work settings. They do not enjoy structure or punching a clock. Independence is key, and INTPs will have very little patience for higher-ups or co-workers whose minds they do not respect. For smooth relationships and more positive feedback at work, some INTPs may need to edit some of their negative viewpoints and learn to tolerate those who do not always live up to their unique standards.

## RELATIONSHIPS WITH FAMILY, FRIENDS, CO-WORKERS

INTPs value flawless thinking and communication. They most enjoy relating to others through logic-based, thinking discussion. However, they can also enjoy fine wit and will easily laugh at clever jokes, ideas, and thoughts.

INTPs do not often seek to discuss emotions and feelings. When INTPs are in relationships with people who do value sharing of emotions, those individuals may feel alienated and frustrated by the INTP lack of focus on feelings. For more intimate relationships, some INTPs may need to learn to acknowledge or value others' feelings and be willing to give credence to them.

In many instances INTPs can be very tolerant of a wide range of behavior from their friends, family, or co-workers, especially when they respect and care about them. They are not easily "threatened" and their significant others often experience their relationships with the INTP as respectful, trusting, and flexible.

Some INTPs will need to make an extra effort to extend themselves with social niceties in group or team situations at work. Not seeing the importance of small talk, they may be left out of the information loop. It is important for INTPs to realize that much information does get exchanged during seemingly social conversations!

## EDUCATIONAL PERFORMANCE

INTPs do quite well in educational settings where reading is required. If they are curious about the topic they are reading, they will pursue their knowledge relentlessly. The result will be fine grades, a terrific source of self-esteem.

---

> "I really understand the subjects I'm studying. I feel like I will be able to use the information in the future."

Frequently for INTPs, a connection will develop with their teacher or professor in which their passions and ideas can be discussed. This acknowledgement from a respected teacher helps the INTP feel connected to their education. Without this connection, some INTPs might isolate themselves and become de-motivated.

Because of the INTP's "need to know" they may be so absorbed in a certain topic or class, their other work could be neglected. Some may need to work toward closure in subjects or projects that hold less interest for them.

INTPs enjoy self-directed learning and need little guidance. Using their analytical minds for learning is one of the greatest gifts of the INTP.

## PHYSICAL SELF

Surprisingly, many INTPs enjoy physical and risky challenges in the outer world. Racing, boxing, and mountain climbing are some activities INTPs have been known to pursue. As in their research, INTPs will learn and practice everything they can about an activity they're interested in and will often excel in that activity.

Other INTPs are attracted to individual or one-to-one activities such as golf, biking, or tennis. They are often fun-loving and stimulating exercise/activity partners.

Some INTPs could neglect their physical and health needs in favor of work or intellectual pursuits. A trusted friend or partner can help to encourage them by providing information and/or enthusiasm about the scientific and psychological benefits of health and nutrition.

## EMOTIONAL SELF

Since many INTPs are absorbed in the rational world of thinking, their emotions receive little focus. They will not pay much heed to feelings that crop up—until they become unmanageable. At that time, the INTP may release biting impatience or anger towards others, often surprising them. As with all types, INTPs may need to acknowledge their feelings and not ignore them, while learning ongoing appropriate expression.

INTPs are often their own worst critics, and although some can outwardly seem arrogant, they are often strict perfectionists. For self-esteem enhancement, INTPs will need to accept their own humanity, and allow themselves to be imperfect sometimes.

If an INTP can theoretically see the importance of their own and others' feelings and desires, they will often be more willing to express and talk through issues that occur in the normal course of relationships. If this realization and skill does not occur, they may simply become inaccessible emotionally and physically and bury themselves in doings of the mind while ignoring the heart.

———————————

## "I feel best when I am in control of myself."

## TALKING WITH INTPS

### SELF-ESTEEM ENHANCERS

**When I. . .**

    . . .finished a bike race with my dad.

    . . .win soccer games and bowling tournaments.

. . .successfully performed a flute solo in a high school band concert.

. . .go out by myself and make friends.

. . .had an awesome, powerful year sophomore year in high school. My friends looked up to me.

. . .was proven right at work.

## SELF-ESTEEM DIMINISHERS

**When I. . .**

. . .am unable to follow through on a project I committed myself to.

. . .am trying to accomplish something and I backtrack.

. . .start to compare myself to my peers.

. . .misjudge a situation after shooting my mouth off about it.

. . .don't do what I know I am capable of doing.

. . .am tired and cranky and say something mean and feel bad about what I said.

## ESTP

ESTPs are talkative, action-oriented people who believe variety is the spice of life. They are on-the-spot problem solvers who can quickly observe and analyze a situation and propose a solution. ESTPs enjoy social contact and are often fun-loving. At the same time, they can be very independent and detached from social niceties and imperatives. ESTPs use their senses to engage with all aspects of the physical world.

### PATHWAYS TO COMPETENCE AND SELF-WORTH

### WORK

ESTPs want movement and action at work. They do not want to be mired in procedures or bureaucratic organizational structures. One ESTP mid-manager reports that she will try to find ways around constricting procedures to solve a problem, and then she simply moves on to the next one. For self-esteem at work, ESTPs need a work setting that gives them the freedom to work in this style.

ESTPs react quickly to problems that need to be solved. On a team, they will provide pragmatic here-and-now solutions. It is sometimes difficult for ESTPs to acknowledge process or history in their drive to find solutions. For maximum effectiveness and self-esteem at work, some ESTPs may need to "take a deep breath" and honor the processes expected of those in the organization.

---

"I like to think I'm able to take action, create solutions, and do a great job."

A work setting where there are a variety of tasks, settings, situations and people is a good fit for ESTPs. If there is too much routine or they perceive that their work world is stagnant, they will move on. They might become impatient with slow processes, abstract planning committees, or other work situations that lack immediate results.

ESTPs' co-workers often find them to be fun loving and vivacious. They can be articulate and persuasive about issues that capture their attention, and for self-esteem, their point of view needs to be heard.

Negotiating and mediating are also strengths of ESTPs. They often cut through to core issues of a problem to find workable solutions between both parties and will find this competency quite gratifying. However, some ESTPs may need to learn to stop and consider people's feelings for maximum effectiveness in this area.

## RELATIONSHIPS WITH FAMILY, FRIENDS, CO-WORKERS

ESTPs can be expected to be direct and blunt communicators in relationships. They will speak directly and are unafraid to express their opinions. While some appreciate this straightforward approach, they run the danger of alienating others when situations require diplomacy and sensitivity.

Fun loving excitement is a hallmark of ESTPs. They can be found in the middle of social events or raucously cheering others from the sidelines. This often makes them popular, and they are frequently included in activities because of their gusto.

ESTPs are very independent. They make their own action and speak their own minds. Although relationships are important for self-esteem, ESTPs are often very self-reliant, and if a relationship isn't working, they'll cut their losses and move on. For social support, some ESTPs may need to sensitize themselves to others' reactions and investment in relationships with them.

"I really do want to trust new friends and true friends. I want to depend on them. But if a relationship isn't working for me, I won't just hang in there."

At work, ESTPs holding leadership positions thrive on juggling several balls at once and are actually energized by pressure. Co-workers with different work styles may find that the ESTP style produces stress and anxiety. In certain work settings, ESTPs will need to modulate their quick paced reactions in order to honor others' points of view and differing styles.

## EDUCATIONAL PERFORMANCE

ESTPs best learn by using their senses. Computers, videos, audio, and color are some multisensory learning strategies they can utilize. They most need to see or experience something new rather than to read about it in the abstract.

Because of their pragmatism, ESTPs are often impatient with theories and abstractions. They sometimes have a hard time just sitting still and may become irritated and frustrated with passive listening. For academic success and self-esteem, some ESTPs will need help finding various study strategies and techniques to make material more palpable for them.

ESTPs are quite expert at memorizing facts and procedures. They can systematically commit details to memory that other types often overlook.

At the college level, some ESTPs will have a more difficult time with the theoretical base of certain classes. In fact, they are often a minority as students or professionals in the college setting. If their major requires classes that have practical application, they will be more prone to persist. For educational feelings of competence, once again ESTPs may need assistance in finding practical learning strategies that work for them.

## PHYSICAL SELF

ESTPs do gravitate toward physical activity and, if able, will readily engage in individual or team sports. They will often be robust and fit and derive the self-esteem benefits from physical fitness.

Many ESTPs also appreciate physical appearance and dressing well, in all its details such as color and texture.

ESTPs often like risky physical sports; however if they cannot take part in them, they often have friends who regularly do.

## EMOTIONAL SELF

ESTPs do not often "pay attention" to emotions and feelings, theirs or others'. When under stress, their emotions can overtake them, and they may focus too much on one mistake, one option, or one issue. It is important for them to put their independent style aside in order to talk with someone who can help them see several options and nuances.

In relationships and work with others who have different styles, some ESTPs may find they do not have support. A skill for their own development is to slow down and really hear people's values and concerns. Doing this will help others become more receptive to the ESTP and will increase the support they are willing to give the ESTP.

---

> "I need to take the time to really think about things and see how I can make everything work."

For growth and development, greater appreciation of the bigger picture of a circumstance, and the long-term impact of their and others' feelings will allow ESTPs to be more effective in many life areas.

## TALKING WITH ESTPS

### SELF-ESTEEM ENHANCERS

**When I. . .**

. . .finished my first semester of college. I was two states away from home, paying my own bills. Nobody thought I would succeed. I did!

. . .was told by an adult friend I would have the most success of all my friends.

. . .went for help in therapy.

. . .sold myself and was hired for a position because of my experience and interview skills. My degree is in a field different from the field of my job!

. . .filled out an application for college and filled it out correctly.

### SELF-ESTEEM DIMINISHERS

**When I. . .**

. . .took a job that didn't work out. I couldn't seem to get my colleagues to understand me.

. . .felt alone and scared when my grandmother died.

. . .received a C for the whole semester.

. . .was left out of a friend's get-together.

. . .shoplifted for something to do. I knew it was wrong. I let a friend put something in my pocket he wanted.

. . .had a complaint filed against me by someone I supervised.

# ESFP

ESFPs enthusiastically embrace the world and its experiences. They enjoy meeting people, having fun with them, and helping others. They also can be skilled peacemakers, troubleshooters, and negotiators because of their ability to cut through extraneous information and clearly see the issues and events in a situation. ESFPs are generous, spontaneous, and realistic. They appreciate what is happening in each of life's moments.

## PATHWAYS TO COMPETENCE AND SELF-WORTH

### WORK

ESFPs feel competent when they are involved in positive events at the work place. One ESFP educational director could frequently be found chairing committees, coordinating events, or serving as master of ceremonies for special occasions.

ESFPs want to make a difference in service to people. Whether it be clients, employees, students, or co-workers, they can excel in playing an important role in problem-solving, training, teaching, or serving as ombudsmen.

Because of the ESFP's friendliness and positive attitude, they seek out contact with people and will create friendly interactions if they are not occurring frequently enough.

ESFPs may sometimes need to force themselves to focus on planning and time management skills because they thrive on interaction with people and their environment. This extraverted energy for people and the environment sometimes detracts from work tasks.

ESFPs can be easily wounded by disapproval and by those individuals who lack appreciation for their enthusiasm. It is important for self-esteem that ESFPs emotionally detach from those individuals. Furthermore, ESFPs need to be careful to seek work environments where others recognize their style as beneficial to the organization, or their self-esteem can suffer from lack of appreciation.

---

## "I feel great at work when I complete everything that needs to be done and everyone is satisfied with my performance."

Although ESFPs enjoy working on and are welcome members of teams and committees, they often express impatience with abstract discussions focusing on theory. Some ESFPs may tune out in these situations, instead of verbally sharing their unique and valuable perspectives

### RELATIONSHIPS WITH FAMILY, FRIENDS, CO-WORKERS

ESFPs are warm, affectionate, and spontaneous, and most other people enjoy their company. Additionally, because of their unpredictable humor and fun-loving nature, they usually have no problem attracting people to them.

---

## "I feel best in relationships when there is real communication going on, lots of mutual support, and no tension."

If ESFPs are not provided with the affection and attention they enjoy (and will return) they may be deeply hurt. It is important for them to learn selectivity in their energy and generosity. They need to be around those who truly appreciate them.

ESFPs may need to look more carefully at the long-term consequences of their spontaneous humor and actions. In the workplace for example, some may misinterpret their fun-loving nature as too easygoing. Additionally, their outgoing and affectionate style could transmit mixed signals to those who may not know them well. Occasionally, their sense of humor will fall flat if the other person wants to have a serious discussion.

Friends and family know they can count on the ESFP. However, they need to be careful to prioritize their time and not to overcommit favors. Some ESFPs need to be careful that others do not use them. Because of their generosity of spirit, others might take them for granted.

## EDUCATIONAL PERFORMANCE

ESFPs enjoy hands-on, practical learning. Theories are much less interesting to them than real-world historical events peopled by interesting characters. They enjoy learning that can be applied immediately to their surroundings or work settings.

ESFPs tend to excel at facts, details, and memories of events. If a test requires recall of this kind of information, they will often earn high grades. Dates, names, colors, numbers will stay in the mind of the ESFP. They enjoy and do well in games such as Jeopardy, Trivial Pursuit, and Scrabble.

ESFPs are often willing to ask questions and make comments to their teachers. Asking questions not only allow ESFPs to create action in their educational setting, it also allows them to humanly connect with the teacher. However, some ESFPs need to learn patience if they are required to listen for long periods.

ESFPs' easy-going nature helps them to enjoy the educational process as it unfolds. Some ESFPs may need to adapt time management and organizational skills in order to meet deadlines and reduce stress.

## PHYSICAL SELF

ESFPs tend to be very connected to their physical selves, and therefore have little problem with exercise as long as there is some fun involved. Fun often includes exercising with other people.

ESFPs enjoy getting outside for physical activity. Others around them may think the weather is so-so, but ESFPs will talk about what a beautiful day it is and encourage their friends or family to join them.

Formal or informal team sports are great sources of self-esteem for ESFPs. They tend to play hard, have fun, and thrive on the people connection inherent in such activities. If they are physically unable to participate, they will happily cheer for others.

## EMOTIONAL SELF

ESFPs are pleasant company and therefore receive lots of positive strokes from their environment. However, if they sense disapproval, they may become encumbered. Either they try too hard to gain approval, or they become deeply hurt or dejected. With maturity, they can learn to read people a bit more cautiously to determine with whom to share their gifts.

---

## "I enjoy making people laugh!"

If relationships become too complex or demanding, ESFPs could retreat from them. They may need to learn to persevere when their friends or partners want to engage in a serious conversation.

Most ESFPs interact quite competently with people and the environment. For continued personal growth and insight, ESFPs need to honor their internal processes and allow time for introspection and self-renewal.

## TALKING WITH ESFPS

### SELF-ESTEEM ENHANCERS

When I. . .

. . .think of all the people I've helped in my life with all the time and money I have given to the needy.

. . .consider many depressing things have happened to me and how I've been able to pick myself up with the help of my friends and improve my life.

. . .help others.

. . .decided to come back to school and take care of my family.

. . .am with my family.

. . .gave a presentation at work and my colleagues praised and congratulated me.

## SELF-ESTEEM DIMINISHERS...

**When I. . .**

. . .feel unappreciated.

. . .am insulted or put down by someone I care about or love.

. . .feel that I haven't performed well on a job and my boss communicates that.

. . .am not heard or acknowledged for what I say.

. . .take things people say to heart.

. . .disappoint people with my decision

# ENFP

ENFPs are energetic, enthusiastic explorers of life. They are excited about exploring the myriad of subjects that capture their imagination. ENFPs generate enthusiasm when they are with others and are positive and supportive of family and friends. ENFPs like to pursue their dreams and need flexibility and freedom from structure in order to do so.

## PATHWAYS TO COMPETENCE AND SELF-WORTH

## WORK

ENFPs contribute creative energy at work. They are often upbeat and supportive in team meetings, office conversations, and as supervisors and supervisees. For self-esteem, they will need to work in an environment valuing their positive focus on ideas and people.

ENFPs need and desire little routine and structure in their work and do not want to be boxed in by too much structure and direction. If they can discover a new way of approaching a problem, they will implement it. ENFPs need freedom to follow their enthusiasms for work to enhance their self-esteem.

Many ENFPs find that work for the betterment of people is a rewarding career path. ENFPs need to feel they are having a positive impact on individuals and even society in general. Many ENFPs would quickly become unhappy if a job contradicts this value.

If a job does not provide enough variety, ENFPs will create it. From developing a specialized expertise, serving on committees or starting special projects, ENFPs seem to have boundless spirit for change and the betterment of the cause. However, some ENFPs may need to manage taking on too many projects with no practical way of completing them.

## "It's important that I do a good job that has an impact, and that someone recognizes me for it."

ENFPs want their co-workers to get along. They will naturally notice common areas of agreement among others and will find ways to bridge disagreements. ENFPs can be effective negotiators and conflict managers and will derive heightened self-esteem from smoothing disagreements and keeping the peace. However, development of their objective thinking processes can help them from becoming too invested in creating harmony.

### RELATIONSHIPS WITH FAMILY, FRIENDS, CO-WORKERS

Most ENFPs have little trouble making connections with people. They make extra effort to stay in touch and therefore create a far-reaching network of personal and professional contacts. Because they are so positive, others usually welcome their calls, and their network for self-esteem support can be extensive.

ENFPs are quite affectionate in their relationships, as well as positive and supportive. They personify many of the qualities that most friends enjoy and have little trouble attracting people.

Because of the very giving quality of ENFPs, some may need to protect themselves emotionally when they do not seem to be getting at least some measure of the support and love they are emitting. ENFPs can become deeply hurt when it dawns on them that their efforts are taken for granted or even unnoticed.

Most ENFPs have no boundaries for their love and caring. From small children to the elderly and people of all shapes, sizes, and colors will benefit from connections with them.

## EDUCATIONAL PERFORMANCE

The ENFPs' openness extends to their learning style. If a subject captures the imagination of an ENFP, he or she will energetically seek to know all they can about it and become quite expert. They can derive self-esteem from the satisfying depth and breadth of knowledge they acquire and are often on the cutting edge of many new developments in their fields.

Because of the people focus of ENFPs, they will seek connections with their teachers, other students, and the material they are learning. ENFPs usually have high verbal skills and are thus able to readily discuss and give reports on their subjects. Talking out their learning is key.

---

*"I study hard and am prepared for testing and discussions. Because I'm so excited by school, I think I help my friends do better when we study together."*

ENFPs may need to learn some prioritization and time management skills. They often work in bursts of energy and sometimes turn in assignments under the wire; they may miss important factual information for their work. To maintain their academic standing, they might need to put in extra effort toward structured details even though these aren't as enjoyable for ENFPs.

## PHYSICAL SELF

Taking care of fitness needs works best for ENFPs if there is a partner or group to exercise with. One ENFP took up jogging with her boss over lunch! She took care of herself physically while fulfilling her social/work needs.

Some ENFPs will overeat or neglect to eat regularly. They may zestfully enjoy food so much that weight problems ensue. For self-esteem as related to body image, ENFPs may need to make a concerted effort to manage their exercise/nutrition. A trusted friend or group to help them with this process is very important.

It is also important for ENFPs to pay attention to ailments that occur. Their outward directed energy on people and the world might cause them to lose focus on what their bodies are telling them. Self-care for self-esteem is crucial.

### EMOTIONAL SELF

ENFPs outwardly express the full continuum of positive feelings and emotions. They are quite demonstrative.

Self-esteem suffers for ENFPs if bureaucracies, or what they perceive as nit-picking people, stymie their values or ideas. ENFPs will often isolate and withdraw if they detect a "brick wall" going up. To regain equilibrium, it is important to ask for support from trusted others who can help them with details and strategies.

For enhanced self-esteem, ENFPs should take time to prioritize their time and values. They need to be careful of overextending, and others can feel resentment from either having to "clean-up" after them or perceiving that the ENFP has not followed through as promised. Feeling negativity from others can be devastating for ENFPs so the process of prioritizing and learning to say "no" is crucial.

---

> "I am at my best when work, play, and recreation all click and everything seems to be going smoothly. I see the positive sides of me."

### TALKING WITH ENFPS

### SELF-ESTEEM ENHANCERS
When I . . .

. . .have stuck to a diet and exercise program and manage to lose weight.

. . .have created new teaching material and the students catch on.

. . .am doing something of some type of service project for other people.

. . .got employee of the month at a restaurant I worked at.

. . .am told by strangers that I have a nice smile.

. . .was told by my manager at work that my best friend and I are their top employees, and worth more than we make.

## SELF-ESTEEM DIMINISHERS

**When I. . .**

. . .am dumped.

. . .stay home a lot.

. . .am not called back or written back.

. . .am not doing anything or any type of service for other people.

. . .am sitting at home for long periods of time and watching television shows.

. . .feel people don't appreciate me for being "me" and try to change me.

# ENTP

ENTPs are enthusiastic pursuers of ideas and possibilities, and enjoy creating unique models and theories. Their breadth and depth of knowledge is usually far-reaching. ENTPs are energized by discussions and debate with other people, and they often provide intellectual leadership because of their ability to analyze and critique almost any situation that occurs.

## PATHWAYS TO COMPETENCE AND SELF-WORTH

### WORK

ENTPs provide astute perspectives on problems to be solved in the workplace. They enjoy perceiving disparate aspects of an issue and then finding a strategy to pull a solution together.

---

> "It's great to lead my fellow workers on a successful day."

New responsibilities and projects keep ENTPs stimulated. They tend to juggle many assignments and are entrepreneurial in their natural discovery of opportunity and unique approaches.

ENTPs are quite persuasive when they want to sell a solution they feel strongly about. They also enjoy a "meeting of the minds" and can be quite open to the input of other people, especially when they hold a high regard for their thinking skills.

Because ENTPs are so focused on overview and conceptual framework and can become overextended, they may overlook details or forget to follow through on steps. For professional recognition, ENTPs need to develop those skills, or seek co-workers who possess these skills for a balanced team approach.

ENTPs need freedom at work from lock-step schedules, bureaucracies, and heavy supervision. Some ENTPs are able to find alternative employment to circumvent these constraints. However, other ENTPs may need to find work situations where they are permitted to work in and be appreciated for their less structured style.

## RELATIONSHIPS WITH FAMILY, FRIENDS, CO-WORKERS

ENTPs are stimulated by other people; they seek out the company of others for discussions and leisure time pursuits. They tend to be quite sociable.

ENTPs prefer people whose minds or outer world accomplishments they respect. They are attracted to the possibilities and the subsequent banter or intellectual interplay that often occurs when a group of people gathers. One ENTP leader enjoys inviting work colleagues to his cabin in the mountains for retreats, planning sessions, or simply to relax.

At work and at home, because ENTPs are less adept with details and follow-through, they often seek companions, employees, or co-workers who will take care of these areas. As long as ENTPs express their appreciation for these qualities in others, this arrangement can work. However, some individuals may become resentful if there is a feeling that they need to frequently "cleanup" after ENTPs.

ENTPs make sought-after confidants. Because of their ability to problem solve, they can often offer solutions to a range of concerns people bring to them, even those of an emotional nature. ENTPs can be very empathic when the situation calls for it.

## EDUCATIONAL PERFORMANCE

ENTPs are terrific students of theories and concepts and enjoy applying their creativity as well as logical thinking in the educational setting. They usually enjoy the process of gathering and gaining new knowledge and are quite stimulated by educational environments. ENTPs are natural, autonomous seekers of knowledge.

ENTPs learn well through verbalizing ideas in discussions, study groups, and debates. They are not averse to verbal sparring and usually gain recognition, and thus self-esteem, because of their fine verbal analysis of a topic.

---

"It's OK when we manage to agree on important issues and agree to disagree on trivial manners."

ENTPs may have difficulty meeting multiple deadlines since their energy for learning takes them in many different time-consuming directions. Some more mature, experienced ENTPs can energetically pull their disparate visions together. However, ENTPs with less experience and skill may not perform as well academically if they lack some time management skills.

ENTPs can overlook supporting details in their pursuit and interest of big picture connections. For further academic success and self-esteem, ENTPs need to develop study strategies that incorporate details.

## PHYSICAL SELF

ENTPs do enjoy physical pursuits and like to play. They value their leisure time, and, fitness goals may be incorporated into their leisure through activities such as hiking, jogging, or even team sports.

If ENTPs become overextended, their leisure time may shrink and their physical self-care will suffer.

ENTPs can find themselves exhausted or even ill because of their tendency to be involved in too much. For this reason, it is important for ENTPs to prioritize their responsibilities, and healthy eating and exercise habits need to be high on that list.

## EMOTIONAL SELF

ENTPs are naturally assertive. They are direct in making their ideas and thoughts known, as well as asking for and promoting what they want. These are healthy self-care behaviors.

In the feeling realm, some ENTPs may need to learn to express positive feelings toward others (since they naturally critique) and to notice the increased intimacy and quality of their relationships with others when this happens.

---

## "My self-esteem is high when I have confidence in what I've accomplished."

As ENTPs mature and develop, introspective activities such as meditation or spiritual pursuits will keep their focus and energy balanced. If these skills are neglected, ENTPs under stress could withdraw into a self-critical, depressive mode.

### TALKING WITH ENTPS

#### SELF-ESTEEM ENHANCERS

When I. . .

>. . .have been a single parent starting over.

>. . .authored an article.

>. . .got promoted and got a raise.

>. . .jumped out of a plane.

>. . .worked in the desert with four strangers for a month.

>. . .wrote and was awarded a large computer hardware grant that benefited the entire school.

#### SELF-ESTEEM DIMINISHERS

When I. . .

>. . .am treated unfairly.

>. . .am not consulted on decisions even if they affect me.

>. . .think about my marriage-highest high, lowest low.

. . .was teased as a kid and called names (I had ADD [Attention Deficit Disorder]). Rejection hurt. Now as an adult in sales, I'm rejected all of the time and it's just part of the job.

. . .am told by people that my faults are worse than I think they are.

. . .can't grasp certain things at school as fast as I think I should.

# ESTJ

ESTJs are organized, planful achievers of goals they set for themselves, their projects, or other people. They will systematically and expediently develop action plans and then thoroughly and single-mindedly bring those plans to completion and fruition. ESTJs are usually quite verbal, with strong opinions based on working traditions and proven past methods.

## PATHWAYS TO COMPETENCE AND SELF-WORTH

### WORK

ESTJs are systematically focused on any job that needs doing and will thoroughly plan how the job needs to be done. Then, without fail, they can be counted on to do it. They achieve a strong sense of satisfaction and self-esteem from completion.

> "I get to make decisions within my scope. I'm proud that things get completed."

ESTJs are natural managers, directors, and leaders. They are able to specifically calculate and develop a plan, and they are usually quite verbal and articulate in communicating that plan for others to follow. They are unafraid of setting the course.

ESTJs are respectful of past practices and will perceive the evidence of what has worked. One ESTJ's ongoing motto is: "If it ain't broke, don't fix it." They see no reason to make changes unless they perceive a logical justification.

Self-esteem is derived by ESTJs when they've made their mark. They enjoy observing and receiving feedback about their accomplishments. They are usually not reluctant to take credit when it is due, again out of logic and fairness. The facts speak for themselves!

ESTJs drive to completion can sometimes interfere with others' needs for latitude and feeling invested in a project through making their own contributions. For support and optimum competence, some ESTJs may need to learn to listen to various points of view, other ways to do a task, and delay decision-making.

## RELATIONSHIPS WITH FAMILY, FRIENDS, CO-WORKERS

ESTJs can usually be counted on to do what is right in relationships. They will "be there" for the people they care about, and they will derive self-esteem from doing something for others that is valuable and important.

ESTJs are also reliable advice-givers. They can often analyze a problem and boil it down to a sensible solution. They are frequently sought after for this skill.

---

## "I think what I express helps me and it frequently helps other people."

ESTJs usually have acute social skills and can be friendly and positive. They are goal-directed even in their social interactions. ESTJs keep small talk to a minimum if there is a goal to be achieved, something to do, or a job to be done.

Because of their strongly held opinions and values, ESTJs can be overpowering with their recommendations about the right way to do things, and what they think is best for others. This can sometimes lead to hurt feelings. Others may perceive lack of respect and listening skills on the part of the ESTJ. Developing their feeling function can help ESTJs focus on what they care about and others' feelings and perspectives.

## EDUCATION OR INTELLIGENCE

ESTJs are pragmatic students. They will learn a lesson thoroughly and doggedly because they know it has to be done. They then proceed to the next step of their educational process.

ESTJs need to know what the teacher expects, and usually are unafraid to ask questions and clarify any assignment. They are uncomfortable and impatient with ambiguous directions or irrelevant assignments. For self-esteem and management of frustration tolerance, some ESTJs will need to develop the skill of living with ambiguity.

Practical applications, hands-on lessons, and material that can later be put to use toward their goals are some ways that ESTJs learn best. They also like to talk out new material with teachers, a study partner, or in study groups.

---

### "I get *A*s and high *B*s. Teachers remember my name and acknowledge me."

ESTJs are usually quite good with procedures and details. They are often skilled at committing this type of material to memory. Sometimes big picture connections and nuances are overlooked entirely, and performance can suffer. Since good grades are important to all types, it is critical for ESTJs to use their intuition to make connections or find a study partner to provide that point of view.

## PHYSICAL SELF

The ESTJ *modus operandi* is to set a goal and achieve it. This style will carry into the health realm. If an ESTJ feels it is important to stay in shape, for example, they will schedule time for their fitness activity and that is when it will get done.

Competition often drives ESTJs. Competitive sports events, or even quantifying how many blocks they walk each day, will be enough for motivated ESTJs to take care of themselves.

Because some ESTJs do overcommit (and it is a rare ESTJ who won't carry out their commitments), other ambitions and responsibilities might lead them to neglect their physical, mental, or nutritional health. Ignoring those areas can set the ESTJ back.

## EMOTIONAL SELF

The outer-directedness of the ESTJ often leaves little time for introspection. ESTJs will tend to compartmentalize or rationalize feelings away, and continue to stay on course, not allowing discomfort to stymie their goals.

If they are ignored for too long, ESTJs sometimes release emotional outbursts, which can be quite surprising, cutting, and do great damage to the other person who has been taken by surprise.

For optimal emotional health, wholeness, and self-esteem growth, ESTJs can learn to ask for help from someone they respect or trust. Greater intimacy and growth can occur for ESTJs when they let down their guard to reveal and examine vulnerable feelings.

## TALKING WITH ESTJS

### SELF-ESTEEM ENHANCERS

When I. . .

> . . .was considered for a position at work that is usually not offered to someone who has been there for less than five years.

> . . .met a high-pressure deadline at work. I felt pretty good about meeting that challenge.

> . . .am recognized by people on my team.

> . . .am able to really "make my mark" on the outcome of something

> . . .hear that my family is proud of my accomplishments.

> . . .was nominated homecoming queen out of all the students in 10th grade

## SELF-ESTEEM DIMINISHERS

**When I. . .**

> . . .get aggressive.

> . . .don't get my plans done in the day they are on my itinerary.

> . . .get second guessed.

> . . .go out with friends and I feel like I don't look good enough or as good as they do.

> . . .get down on myself after a sports competition. It is hard to get motivated again.

> . . .disappoint someone I care about.

# ESFJ

ESFJs are active and people oriented. They enjoy accomplishing tasks in service to and with other people. They are friendly, energetic, and fun-loving, yet they are focused on making things happen in the outer world. ESFJs are sensitive to others' needs and can be emotionally sensitive themselves; they are sometimes easily hurt. They are often traditional, from observing the values and customs of their workplace to ensuring that family holidays and traditions are acknowledged and observed.

## PATHWAYS TO COMPETENCE AND SELF-WORTH

### WORK

ESFJs work best with people, especially on tasks and projects that produce tangible benefits for their co-workers, customers, or clients. Watching people benefit from their efforts helps ESFJs feel competent and worthy.

ESFJs excel in organizing and seeing projects through to their successful conclusions. Most events or projects do not daunt ESFJs. They are excellent orchestrators and motivators of events and people, and they can be held in high regard for their abilities in this area.

ESFJs are decisive; they want to and often will lead their team to immediate action. Because of their natural need to move, they may need to learn greater patience with bureaucracies or procedures and timelines under which they have little or no control. On the other hand, they can be very effective and forceful in circumventing those kinds of obstacles that may have stopped others.

Harmony is of great importance to ESFJs, and they often go to great lengths to keep the peace at work. Co-workers often confide in ESFJs and ask for their pragmatic and action-oriented counsel.

> "I like to accomplish something at work that
> I feel needs to be changed or improved.
> I like being praised for that."

ESFJs are highly in tune to the feelings and reactions of their co-workers, and this sensitivity is appreciated by others. On the other hand, sensitivity sometimes leads ESFJs to overpersonalize or overreact to even mild forms of negative criticism. Some ESFJs may need to develop their objective, thinking based perspectives when these situations occur.

## RELATIONSHIPS WITH FAMILY, FRIENDS, CO-WORKERS

ESFJs have many friends and are loyal to the people they care about in their lives. They are involved in relationships, from the commemorative greeting card to the special birthday party (including favorite decor, menu, and presents for the lucky birthday person).

Family and friends will regularly call upon ESFJs for help, and ESFJs will often develop immediate and tangible solutions to the problems of others. However, ESFJs can sometimes be too quick to fix a situation for their friends, co-workers, or family, without checking out if their solution is really what the person wanted or needed.

> "I am content when everyone is happy and
> there are no major problems."

ESFJs frequently avoid discord in relationships. Positive feelings are to be nurtured and negative ones are often ignored. Many ESFJs hold a strong sense of values. If they perceive (accurately or not) that someone they care about has "crossed the line'" they may avoid that person or even sever the relationship. For self-esteem, the ESFJ may need to seek other points of view about what occurred, before assuming negative intentions.

# "It's important to talk out my feelings and be told it's OK."

ESFJs like to have fun. They are usually in the middle of the action, and they laugh easily, often seeing the humor in situations. They will feel great about themselves as they notice others appreciating their contribution to the group.

## EDUCATIONAL PERFORMANCE

ESFJs are conscientious learners and often do quite well due to their natural planning and follow-through. These self-management skills for school often result in good grades, contributing to self-esteem.

They learn best when they can relate their studies to experiences they have had or at least see the practical application of their learning.

ESFJs like to talk through their new knowledge to process it. If they feel they are in a safe, supportive environment, they will have much to contribute verbally to the educational experience through discussions and small group work.

ESFJs need to connect to individuals within their educational experience for fulfillment to occur. This connection can happen with the instructor, in a study group, or even with material they can personalize. Some ESFJ students may need to learn to tolerate learning experiences that seem highly theoretical. One way to do this is by having someone they trust point out the reason for or relevance of what they are learning.

## PHYSICAL SELF

In sports or fitness-related activities, ESFJs will choose those in which they can connect with others. They will join company softball teams or participate in hikes or other group physical activities. Many ESFJs ski or roller blade with their friends and families. To take care of their bodies and relieve stress, connecting with other people is a key motivator.

Fitness is fun for ESFJs. They may do aerobics or aerobic dance after work. One ESFJ woman became friends with her instructors and co-exercisers and often planned and organized dinner parties after class.

ESFJs will whole-heartedly embrace nutritional or fitness goals. Sometimes they may latch onto or overindulge in these pursuits if they allow themselves to get swept up in them.

## EMOTIONAL SELF

Emotions run high for ESFJs. They enjoy people to their fullest and will enthusiastically create situations where good feelings and harmony occur. They derive great satisfaction from contributing to others' happiness, and this is a source of self-esteem for them.

ESFJs need to be recognized for their contributions to relationships and like to be surrounded by people who provide that recognition. However, if ESFJs sense a slight, they may strongly personalize it and be deeply hurt by others. They can jump to faulty conclusions about perceived criticism.

For many ESFJs, a valuable self-esteem builder will be to learn assertive communication. This includes communicating what they need or want, whether or not it is popular, and to learn to ask questions and check out another person's behavior before jumping to conclusions about it. Some ESFJs may also need to learn that it is OK not to please everyone, and in fact that it is virtually impossible to please some people.

## TALKING WITH ESFJS

### SELF-ESTEEM ENHANCERS

When I. . .

> . . .am giving in relationships as well as receiving.

> . . .am both a mother, and I hold a job for a long period of time.

> . . .give advice to friends and I can help them by sharing past or present difficulties.

. . .get report cards with only As and Bs.

. . .am praised by board members.

. . .am chosen to represent my company at conferences and meetings

## SELF-ESTEEM DIMINISHERS

**When I. . .**

. . .am not given credit for things I implement.

. . .think I'm being pushy and not open enough.

. . .make a mistake at work and it affects other people.

. . .am having problems with myself and try to hide everything because I don't think I need anyone's help.

. . .allow my friend not to accept his responsibility when he says he'll call, then I don't tell him my feelings.

. . .am misread.

## ENFJ

ENFJs are friendly, people-centered achievers who thrive on the depth and breadth of the many interests that capture them. They are usually quite competent and able to energetically succeed in pursuing and attaining the visions and goals they set for themselves. ENFJs often have a wide circle of friends, are easy communicators of their values and positive feelings.

## PATHWAYS TO COMPETENCE AND SELF-WORTH

### WORK

ENFJs are skilled jugglers of projects, and they directly ask for involvement of others to help them carry out their visions and goals. The ENFJ, however, will be the visionary and will orchestrate the plan.

Service to people, which is congruent with their respect for humanity, is the driving value behind careers that ENFJs pursue. If the organization's values are a mismatch for the ENFJ, they will seek and usually attain other employment.

ENFJs do not easily give up. They will persistently plan and research ways to bring their vision into the world or assist other people in achieving their goals. Their co-workers appreciate their support and dependability. Some ENFJs may need to work harder at noticing details or, to carry out their vision, enlist the help of a co-worker with that strength.

ENFJs' exuberant enthusiasm and verbal skill provides drive to the group. However, at times they can be perceived as overwhelming and overenthusiastic. Some ENFJs may need to tone it down so that others are not overwhelmed by their energy.

If the ENFJ does not receive feedback and support for the energy and effort they exert, they can become completely opposite of what others are used to seeing. Negativity and hopelessness will overcome them. In that case, a trusted friend with a different point of view may be able to logically analyze the situation with them.

## RELATIONSHIPS WITH FAMILY, FRIENDS, CO-WORKERS

ENFJs tend to have a wide circle of friends since they are compassionate and caring individuals. They are very comfortable approaching people and drawing them out.

---

> "I can easily go up to people and start opening up to them. I love meeting people."

ENFJs are terrific at maintaining relationships with others. Phone calls, cards for special occasions, and email contact are par for the course. People are important to ENFJs, and they will make the time for them.

Others may not have the same energy as the ENFJ for maintaining relationships. Eventually, some ENFJs will re-direct their efforts towards people who appreciate and reciprocate their friendship. For self-esteem, a few ENFJs may need to recognize the need to disengage from relationships that are not mutually satisfying.

Although the ENFJs have strong verbal skills that create a confident front, they can be easily hurt and disappointed by slights in the workplace or from family and friends. Some ENFJs may tend to overreact or dramatize these slights and may need to learn to balance reality with the feeling reactions that could have drawn them to faulty conclusions.

## EDUCATION OR INTELLIGENCE

ENFJs enjoy the educational process, particularly when it involves talking about ideas that are about or improve the lives of people. One ENFJ student describes what she perceives as technical or impersonal classes as "hoops to jump through" toward greater educational goals.

The goal-directedness of ENFJ students will drive them to get assignments done on time. They will spend as much time as necessary completing work that captures their interests.

---

## "I know I am creative and organized; it really shows in my grades."

ENFJs want to connect with teachers and peers. They are motivated by acceptance and approval in the educational setting, and because they are organized and complete their work, are usually able to gain it. However, if they detect disapproval they may simply do the minimum amount in their learning because they are deeply hurt.

ENFJs also can enjoy classes where their inquisitive minds are being stimulated by subject matter. Some ENFJs might want to form study groups or have study partners, especially to assist them with strategies for memorization and sensing details.

## PHYSICAL SELF

ENFJs' energy for people and interaction in the environment helps them to be involved in physical activities in groups. From rollerblading to skiing to softball, ENFJs who are able are usually part of the action.

ENFJs usually look for a partner for jogging, walking, biking, hiking, or other physical activity. To achieve balance between social interaction and solitude, some ENFJs have learned to be OK occasionally doing these activities alone.

Because of their enthusiastic involvement in an abundance of activities through work and play, it is important for ENFJs not to overextend themselves. Playing (and working) long hours with and for people can lead to exhaustion, illness, and injury.

## EMOTIONAL SELF

ENFJs usually handle their emotions quite positively, until they are let down in some way by a person or people they care about. Since they usually seek the silver lining, they can sometimes be over-idealistic. A trusted confidant may be needed to help ENFJs sort objective facts from their emotional reaction to events.

Overlooking of facts can set the ENFJ up for deep disappointment. They may become self-critical if they take someone else's issues too personally and blame themselves for their inability to create a positive relationship.

In highly charged situations or conflicts, some ENFJs tend to use black and white thinking and blanket condemnations of people. Others may be quite surprised at the vehemence in which they discount someone who may not have lived up to their standards or values. For self-esteem development, some ENFJs may need to learn to see gray areas in conflict, and they also need to see that others' points of view are sometimes valuable and valid.

---

"I can now control my people pleasing behaviors."

## TALKING WITH ENFJS

### SELF-ESTEEM ENHANCERS

**When I . . .**

. . .began to excel at what I was doing after a year as a missionary.

. . .received a standing ovation at a concert performance.

. . .excelled in track and field.

. . .began to explain and communicate directly, instead of trying to control and manipulate to get what I want.

. . .am with my family for impromptu together time, a video, board game, or picnic.

. . .reach out to my friends and am really honest and listen to what they're saying.

## SELF-ESTEEM DIMINISHERS

**When I. . .**

> . . .neglect or hurt others.

> . . .am not in good physical shape. I feel less confident and energetic.

> . . .feel 'dim' when I forget something I once knew.

> . . .feel shamed and even overlooked for appreciation and recognition.

> . . .lose patience with my inability to think as fast as other people can. Compare myself too much to others.

> . . .think everyone seems to have something better to do than spend time with me.

## ENTJ

ENTJs are logical, action-oriented leaders. ENTJs want to arrange and re-arrange the outer world to fit their internal vision of what is best and most productive. They enjoy taking charge of most or all aspects of their environment and do so in a most forceful and assertive manner. They seem very confident and well-versed about topics they are discussing.

## PATHWAYS TO COMPETENCE AND SELF-WORTH

### WORK

ENTJs are skilled at analyzing situations and quickly proposing action-oriented solutions. They will strategically chart a course for solving problems of any magnitude. ENTJs derive self-esteem from watching their solutions come to fruition, and they need to be in a work environment that allows them the latitude to serve as directors of action.

---

## "I work best when I feel that I'm in control."

Well-developed ENTJ leaders will hire people who can competently assist them in carrying out their visions of a well-oiled organization. Since they are usually quite confident about their plans, they are not threatened by others' strengths. They are often quite respectful of the unique insights provided by other people regarding their plans.

ENTJs naturally want to orchestrate their workplace, or at least a large part of it. It is unnatural for an ENTJ to work alone, on a small project, or stuck in a "cubby" without others to direct or at least engage in debate or discourse. Without visible or public recognition and results, the ENTJ's self-esteem may begin to suffer.

Planning for the future is a strength of ENTJs. They will strategically think ahead, long before others, and are often able to anticipate problems before they occur. One ENTJ teacher is regularly consulted by administrators as well as peers for his respected perceptions and opinions.

ENTJs need control to carry out their visions. Power and status is also necessary for some ENTJs to feel competent. For self-esteem to occur, ENTJs need to seek work environments where they are able to bring their visions to fruition. For implementation of their ideas, some ENTJs may need to develop a focus on sensing details.

## RELATIONSHIPS WITH FAMILY, FRIENDS, CO-WORKERS

The healthiest and most sustained relationships for ENTJs are those in which the other person exhibits personal strength and expresses their own opinions and feelings. ENTJs respect and welcome these as well as other assertive behaviors from their friends and co-workers. They are energized by the challenge of debate and discussion.

---

> "I always feel good around my friends.
> I enjoy when we're all open
> and able to talk to one another."

ENTJs tend to be highly verbal and expressive. Some ENTJs may need to learn to be more patient with other people's needs to process and think before speaking, and they may need to develop a greater willingness to listen before speaking.

ENTJs bring terrific energy to their interactions with people and often add excitement and fun to human interactions.

In friendships and love relationships, ENTJs have a natural tendency to critique as well as take control. Some ENTJs may need to learn to modulate these behaviors to sustain friendships and let their partners feel like they too have some control of the direction of the partnership. Self-esteem can suffer for ENTJs when others, who feel overpowered, distance themselves from them.

## EDUCATIONAL PERFORMANCE

ENTJs enjoy the learning process and quickly see connections between theories and events. They will often propose their own theories and then develop ways to apply them.

ENTJs learn through action. It is more difficult for some ENTJs to sit still for prolonged study periods, and they learn best when they can verbalize their perceptions and ideas. Therefore, study partners, study groups, and class discussions work well for ENTJs.

Because of ENTJ's large-scale grasp of events and theories, they may overlook facts that either refute or support their visions. For feelings of competence, they may need to learn to focus a bit more on facts and details for higher grades.

ENTJs also possess natural time management skills for school success. They will schedule study times, plan for quizzes and tests, and hand assignments in on time. Their attention to timelines and assignments often receives recognition from the teacher.

---

*"I enjoy reviewing all the goals I have accomplished, what my life is like today, and my very positive future."*

## PHYSICAL SELF

ENTJs' goal driven style is also extended to their pursuit of fitness and attractiveness. Once an ENTJ decides getting fit is a worthy goal for them, they will pursue and quantify weight loss, pounds lifted, or minutes run; they will see results.

Some ENTJs gravitate toward group pursuits like sports or dance troops.

They are frequently team driven and competitive and often take a leadership role.

Physical attractiveness holds an esteemed place in ENTJ's value system. Even though attractiveness is valued in our culture, ENTJs particularly will seek to put their best selves forward because it will further their goals.

## EMOTIONAL SELF

ENTJs can be slow at acknowledging internal stress and will often discount any gnawing discomfort. For full personal development and self-esteem, many ENTJs will need to learn to listen to and honor uncomfortable feelings.

It is often difficult for ENTJs to show vulnerability or admit mistakes; however, growth and self-esteem can occur when they find a trusted confidant who will accept their vulnerabilities. Additionally, when an ENTJ does show more feelings, positive or negative, they will often earn increased respect from others, and therefore enhance their self-esteem.

ENTJs can have great emotional difficulty when they perceive they have been rejected. For enhanced self-esteem, they may need to be reminded that interactions are not always win/lose, and that whether it is a personality conflict or just plain lack of "chemistry," not all relationships develop the way they want them to.

## TALKING WITH ENTJS

### SELF-ESTEEM ENHANCERS

**When I. . .**

> . . .attained my first job without anyone's assistance.

> . . .look at all of the projects at work that I know I had a hand in starting.

> . . .gave my public speech for the first time, in front of people I barely knew.

> . . .received great grades my first year back at school.

> . . .stood up for myself in a courtroom.

> . . .play with the stock market and make money.

## SELF-ESTEEM DIMINISHERS

**When I. . .**

. . .have put in extra work that was required of me, and people do not recognize that.

. . .am talked down to.

. . .have to give up something I want to do personally.

. . .am treated by my family like I don't know what I'm talking about.

. . .don't ask questions at school about material I don't understand.

. . .am not doing as well as everyone else.

# PART THREE

# GUIDELINES FOR ENHANCING SELF-ESTEEM

## THE GIFT OF SELF-KNOWLEDGE THROUGH TYPE KNOWLEDGE

A critical tool for self-esteem enhancement is to know yourself: your strengths, weaknesses, likes, and dislikes. Through self-knowledge we appreciate ourselves, and all of our human gifts and failings. Personal growth is a lifelong journey and an ever-changing process. People with high self-esteem are willing to change and improve and to accept aspects of themselves that are "imperfect."

Type knowledge through the MBTI is a magnificent tool for self-knowledge and acceptance. Self-understanding through type knowledge addresses both facets of the self-esteem definition: competence and self-worth. As we realize our type preferences and strengths, especially in the competence domains of work, education, relationships, physical self, and emotional self, we can capitalize on them. Then we can explore the typical blind spots of our type in those areas and learn mental and behavioral adjustments for acceptance or improvement.

Self-worth starts with early experiences of parental acceptance of our uniqueness and individual personality style. If this did not occur in our formative years, we may now be carrying negative messages about who we are, even if we were simply different from other members of our family.

As adults, type consciousness reveals that our personality differences, in reality, do not have to be "overcome." We do have the choice to surround ourselves as much as possible with people who accept our personalities. The way we are energized, perceive, decide, and live our outer lives may be different from our neighbor, spouse, co-worker, and children. And that is OK!!

To glean the most about type and self-esteem beyond this publication, refer to the list of resources (p. 117). The more we know, the more we grow.

## OTHER TOOLS FOR SELF-ESTEEM ENHANCEMENT

The tools listed below provide just a few ideas and guidelines for self-esteem enhancement. Not meant to be exhaustive, they are ideas for further exploration, and a starting place for deciding where to focus change.

**Monitoring Self-Talk**. Negative mind chatter and a frequent or steady stream of internal self-criticism ("you blew it again, "what an idiot," "why can't you be like. . ."), keeps individuals with low-self esteem from practicing new behaviors and from achieving high self-esteem. If we are constantly punishing and berating ourselves in our heads when we make mistakes or fail in some way, we are programming ourselves to avoid situations that might lead to personal growth. Personal development and therefore self-esteem cannot occur.

The "internal bully" is a habit that requires modification, because what we tell ourselves is what we believe about ourselves—whether our self-talk is good, bad, or indifferent. Assistance from a counselor or teacher will help to minimize or eliminate negative self-talk. In turn, replacing your self-talk with positive statements ("I did my best," "I'm a competent person," "I learned a lot from that") will lead to increased self-esteem.

**Risk-Taking**. Risk-taking involves learning to push oneself to try behaviors that are new and uncomfortable. It then includes the realization that imperfect outcomes or failed plans do not mean total personal failure. Through risk taking, we can practice then achieve new competencies. When we do learn new skills, our self-esteem improves!

One person's risk is different from the next person's, and our individual risks can range anywhere from making a phone call to someone we admire, to taking a class, to saying "no" to a request we do not really have time to fulfill. The important fact for self-esteem enhancement is that we try something different, stretch ourselves, and then mentally reward ourselves for trying. Positive internal rewards should come for risking whether the outcome is success, failure, or somewhere in between.

**Giving to Others/Contributing**. Contrary to some popular notions, increased self-esteem does not equate to selfishness! As a matter of fact, people with high self-esteem realize they have strengths, time, or knowledge to contribute. Through giving, they know that in their special ways, their contributions are meaningful. Competency and self-worth are thus enhanced.

In contrast, people with low self-esteem often are disconnected from the joy of helping others who are less fortunate. They may devalue the impact of their potential contributions. For self-esteem enhancement, finding ways to help others directly—from reading to a child or children, volunteering with the elderly, or even stuffing envelopes for an organization whose cause you believe in—takes us outside of ourselves and enhances self-esteem. We see our value in our own special way and in our particular niche in the world.

**Assertiveness**. Simply put, assertiveness is healthy communication. It means taking what we feel inside, finding the words, and expressing them: honestly, appropriately, respectfully, and directly. Assertiveness links back to knowing ourselves and honoring how we feel (not waiting to see what others' feel or think, i.e., codependency).

Assertiveness is a skill to be learned. For Introverts, it may mean an adjustment from a tendency to keep self-expression internal. For Extraverts, modifying self-expression to learn to listen and process a bit more prior to speaking could be helpful. Ultimately, assertiveness does benefit all types' self-esteem. It is simply a behavior of self-respect, while respecting others.

**Physical fitness, nutrition and health**. Self-care is a self-esteem behavior. Eating disorders and neglect of physical fitness can create a negative feedback loop. If physical self-image is negative, then self-esteem is lowered. If self-esteem is lowered, then self-care suffers. The solution lies in small steps toward enhanced health empowerment. Support groups, exercise partners, even medical consultation can serve, for all types, to motivate toward reaching these goals.

**Counseling, bibliotherapy, personal growth classes.** To further reach self-understanding and appreciation, counseling with a qualified therapist is often in order. Even a few sessions can shed light on areas for focusing personal change. Additionally, community colleges or continuing education programs often offer classes for personal growth and physical and nutritional fitness. Self-help books, wisely chosen or recommended by professionals, can also serve as a source of inspiration and behavioral change.

## PHILLIP'S STORY: A HAPPY ENDING

*Phillip finally sought counseling from his community college counselor. Through the therapeutic process, he learned to "diversify" his sources of self-esteem. Phillip realized he should not let any person determine his OKness, and that he needed to become involved with activities on campus to meet people and gain other sources of self-worth and feelings of competence.*

*From taking the MBTI, Phillip had an enlightening "aha" experience about the mismatch of his job to his personality type. He learned that not mastering his customer service job had nothing to do with intelligence and everything to do with a mismatch of skills. Fortunately, Phillip applied for and was offered a job as a peer helper at the high school outreach office of his college. There, he could work individually with high school students, helping them to understand the process of starting college. Phillip "shined" in this job.*

*An avid reader, Phillip devoured books about assertiveness recommended by his counselor. With his counselor's guidance and his reading and behavioral prac-tice, Phillip recognized how important it was for his mental health to express his feelings (even negative ones). He learned to ask for information and clarification, especially in dating relationships.*

*Through self-exploration over two semesters, Phillip began to like himself more. He gained self-worth and competence and new tools to handle life's challenges as they occurred.*

# FURTHER RESOURCES

*Antecedents of Self-Esteem* by Stanley Coopersmith. Palo Alto, CA: Consulting Psychologists Press, 1967.

*Building Self-Esteem* by Bonnie J. Golden and Kay Lesh. Upper Saddle River, New Jersey: Prentice-Hall, 1997.

*"Causes, Correlates, and the Functional role of Global Self-Worth: A Lifespan Perspective"* by Susan Harter. In *Competence Considered* edited by J. Kolligan and R Sternberg. New Haven: Yale University Press, 1989.

*Do What You Are* by Paul D. Tieger and Barbara Barron-Tieger. New York: Little, Brown and Company, 1995.

*Intimacy and Type* by Jane Hardy Jones and Ruth G. Sherman, Gainesville FL: Center for Applications of Psychological Type., 1997.

*Lifetypes* by Sandra Krebs Hirsh and Jean M Kummerow. New York: Warner Books, 1989.

*Looking at Type and Learning Styles.* by Gordon Lawrence. Gainesville, FL: Center for Applications of Psychological Type, 1997.

*Looking at Type in the Workplace* by Larry Demarest. Gainesville, FL: Center for Applications of Psychological Type, 1997.

*Looking at Type: The Fundamentals* by Charles Martin. Gainesville, FL: Center for Applications of Psychological Type, 1997.

*Self-Esteem* by Matthew Mckay, and Patrick Fanning. Oakland, CA: New Harbinger Publications, 1987.

*Self-Esteem and Psychological Type: Definitions, Interactions, and Expressions* by Bonnie J. Golden. Gainesville, Fl: Center for Applications of Psychological Type, 1994.

*Your Perfect Right* by Robert E. Alberti and Michael L. Emmons. San Luis Obispo, CA: Impact Publishers, 1995.

# OTHER BOOKS OF INTEREST

## WORK, PLAY AND TYPE
ACHIEVING BALANCE IN YOUR LIFE

By Judith A. Provost $11.95

 Is your work productive? Do you take time for play? Learn how your work shapes your leisure and how it affects balance or burnout in your life. Examples and case studies illustrate how different types approach work and play, and how you can work toward a healthy balance between the two.

## LOOKING AT TYPE™: THE FUNDAMENTALS

By Charles R. Martin $7.00 each. Quantity discounts available.

 Discover a clearer picture of your personality through a deeper understanding of your Myers-Briggs Type Indicator® results. *The Fundamentals* offers the basics for using type as a dynamic model of personality and lifelong development. Available separately or in packages of 10 for classes and seminars. This is one book in a series that includes:

- *Looking at Type™ and Careers*
- *Looking at Type™ in the Workplace*
- *Looking at Type™ and Spirituality*
- *Looking at Type™ and Learning Styles*

For more information about these books or other CAPT books and products, call for a catalog or visit our website, **www.capt.org**

The Center for Applications of Psychological Type (CAPT) is a nonprofit organization that promotes the accurate understanding, measurement, ethical use, and practical applications of the Myers-Briggs Type Indicator® instrument. CAPT publishes and distributes books about the MBTI® instrument and its applications, produces materials and products for administration; and offers workshops and training programs for qualification and advanced education in administering the Indicator.

2815 NW 13th Street Suite 401 ■ Gainesville FL 32609
800.723.6284